ELEMENTARY AND MIDDLE SCHOOL TEACHERS IN THE MIDST OF REFORM

Common Thread Cases

Traci Bliss
Idaho State University

Joan Mazur
University of Kentucky

with **John Buzzard**

MERRILL,
an imprint of Prentice Hall
Upper Saddle River, New Jersey   *Columbus, Ohio*

Library of Congress Cataloging-in-Publication Data

Bliss, Traci.
    Elementary and middle school teachers in the midst of reform : common thread cases / Traci Bliss, Joan Mazur
       p. cm.
    Includes bibliographical references (p.).
    ISBN 0-13-716474-2
    1. Elementary school teachers--United States--Case studies. 2. Elementary school teaching--United States--Case studies. 3. Middle school teachers--United States--Case studies. 4. Middle school teaching--United States--Case studies. 5. School improvement programs--United States--Case studies. 6. Educational change--United States--Case studies. I. Mazur, Joan. II. Title.

LB1776.2.B45   2000
372.11'0973--dc21   99-046139
                                                                                      CIP

Editor: Debra A. Stollenwerk
Editorial Assistant: Penny S. Burleson
Production Editor: Mary Harlan
Design Coordinator: Diane C. Lorenzo
Text Designer: Melanie N. King
Cover Designer: Ceri Fitzgerald
Cover art: ©SuperStock, Inc.
Production Manager: Pamela D. Bennett
Electronic Text Management: Marilyn Wilson Phelps, Karen L. Bretz, Melanie N. King
Director of Marketing: Kevin Flanagan
Marketing Manager: Meghan Shepherd
Marketing Coordinator: Krista Groshong

This book was set in Novarese by Prentice Hall and was printed and bound by R. R. Donnelley & Sons, Inc. The cover was printed by Phoenix Color Corp.

©2000 by Prentice-Hall, Inc.
Pearson Education
Upper Saddle River, New Jersey 07458

All rights reserved. No part of this book may be reproduced, in any form or by any means, without permission in writing from the publisher.

Photo credits: All images supplied by the authors.

Printed in the United States of America

10 9 8 7 6 5 4 3 2 1

ISBN: 0-13-716474-2

Prentice-Hall International (UK) Limited, *London*
Prentice-Hall of Australia Pty. Limited, *Sydney*
Prentice-Hall of Canada, Inc., *Toronto*
Prentice-Hall Hispanoamericana, S. A., *Mexico*
Prentice-Hall of India Private Limited, *New Delhi*
Prentice-Hall of Japan, Inc., *Tokyo*
Prentice-Hall (Singapore) Pte. Ltd., *Singapore*
Editora Prentice-Hall do Brasil, Ltda., *Rio de Janeiro*

To Caroline Ellington, a continuing source of inspiration.

Elementary and Middle School Teachers in the Midst of Reform: Common Thread Cases was made possible through the generous support of:
  The Bell South Foundation, Atlanta, Georgia
  The Gheens Foundation, Louisville, Kentucky
  Kentucky Educational Television, Lexington, Kentucky

FOREWORD

We have one constant in American education: change. Nowhere is the optimistic, pragmatic American spirit more buoyant than in our constant efforts to reform the public schools. Educational ideas burst into bloom, wither, and are born again. Progressive educational ideas cycle through our educational system in ever-changing incarnations—open classrooms, team teaching, whole-language methods. Traditional education then makes its claim, and the cycle begins again. We are forever "tinkering toward Utopia," as David Tyack and Larry Cuban (1995) so aptly characterize the last century of American school reform.[1] Again, as we move into the millennium, hope and reforms accelerate—technology in the classroom, standards-based teaching, authentic assessment.

The cases in this valuable volume show us what actually happens in classrooms, in schools, and in teachers' personal lives, as they cope with external reforms such as new state standards. But these cases also show us the mistake in the common view that educational reforms are impositions from without, which teachers in the trenches resist and for good reason. As these cases demonstrate, teachers themselves seek out change. Reforms, many say, did not have to be imposed on them. They were already innovating, in the midst of reforms of their own devising, seeking their own renewal.

Educational reform and the problems that change brings will always be with us. The Common Thread Cases provide true-story examples of teachers dealing with the dilemmas of reform. The cases in this volume are chosen to illustrate the range of reforms and their variety (see the Issues Matrix, pp. xviii–xix). At the positive end of the continuum, Common Threads offers "inspirational" cases. "Reading, Writing, and RAM" shows us Vicki Lugo, a teacher who masters her own fears of technology and uses computers not as razzle-dazzle but to achieve literacy. As in the classic heroic epic, this case offers a moral message: "Yes, you are untried . . . moving among powerful, experienced people, some of them malevolent, but you are young, brave, and pure of heart. Take the risk. You are sufficient."

At the opposite end of the continuum, this casebook offers "cautionary" tales, cases of reforms gone wrong. "Caroline Never Smiles" shows us a reform once vital and now ossified and bureaucratized, where educators follow the letter of the law but have lost the spirit. Despite all the individualized education programs, the emphasis on inclusion, and the extensive team meetings, Caroline slips through the safety net that special education policies were supposed to provide. This case poses the classic

---

[1] *Tinkering Toward Utopia: A Century of Public School Reform* (Cambridge: Harvard University Press, 1995).

question: Why does one generation's fervor turn into another generation's formula? Can any educational problem ever be solved, or will reforms always be necessary because *they* renew the spirit?

Reforms also have gone wrong because they were undertaken for the wrong reasons. "Compromise and Defeat" asks us to think about this worry. The principal, Jack Carnes, proposes to change the structure of the middle school with an eye on his own career advantage. This case alerts teachers to the mixture of motives that can underlie pressures toward reform and to the circumstances in which resistance may be justifiable. Common Threads does not make the mistake of assuming that every reform is good and true.

Questions about reform rarely have simple answers. Reforms benefit some but not others, create transition costs, and have uncertain outcomes. Cases are especially well suited to capture such ambiguity, and this volume performs a great service in providing emblematic cases of reform for educators to think through. These cases can help them recognize the pitfalls and the promise of reforms and remind them to approach reform with wisdom and grace.

A special virtue of this project is that CD-ROM cases are available as a companion to the written cases. This technological innovation is on the frontier of case method instruction. The animated narratives and rich visual images enable teachers to experience far greater depth than written narratives alone. The CD-ROM also makes it possible for teachers to engage in on-line discussions about cases and related problems they are experiencing in their own classrooms. They can seek advice and support without revealing personal difficulties that might affect their reputation or tenure. The technology creates a safe environment.

The CD-ROM won the 1996 Outstanding Practice in Instructional Development Award (Association for Educational Communications and Technology). It is an excellent example of technology that supports change and demonstrates how technology is important to reform.

We are a nation of tinkerers, and reform will always be with us. Still, whatever the siren song of the moment, teachers must deal well with the down-to-earth business of teaching their students in their schools. As Rabbi Yohana ben Zakkai says in the Talmud,[2] "If you have a sapling in your hand and are told, 'Look the Messiah is here,' you should first plant the sapling and then go out to welcome the Messiah."

Judith Kleinfeld, professor of psychology, University of Alaska

---

[2]Quoted in *The Book of Legends*, ed. by H. M. Blalik and Y. H. Rabnitzky (New York: Schocken, 1992).

PREFACE

Elementary and Middle School Teachers in the Midst of Reform: Common Thread Cases has a unique focus. This volume, like its predecessor, *Secondary and Middle School Teachers in the Midst of Reform*, presents true stories of innovation, capturing the dilemmas, frustrations, and accomplishments of elementary teachers as they navigate the complex issues of change. The subtitle, "Common Thread Cases," refers to the Interstate New Teacher Assessment and Support Consortium (INTASC) New Teacher Performance Standards that support each case (see the INTASC Standards Matrix on pp. xx–xxi).

PURPOSE OF THE BOOK

The series is designed to be used in both teacher education and teacher professional development contexts. For the beginning teacher, the narratives provide an opportunity to be prepared for the demands of change, especially insofar as those demands are reflected in performance standards. For both the new and experienced teacher, the cases are excellent vehicles for in-depth reflection—what alternative courses of action were available to the teacher featured in the case, and with what consequences? What would I have done under the circumstances, and what theoretical perspectives support my choices? The "Instructor's Quick Guide" (available from the publisher) provides examples of how the cases can be successfully used to support rigorous analysis of salient educational issues and teaching principles reflected in the INTASC standards.

SHARED STRUCTURE OF THE CASES

This series of stories shares a common structure and a consistent theme of change. All of the Common Thread Cases share the following elements:

1. Each story consists of a true, factually correct, compelling account of a teacher's pedagogy in the context of change. Events take place over an extended period of time; consequences of actions as well as unexpected developments are an integral part of the narrative.
2. Within each story, episodes of teaching and learning are portrayed in rich detail. Particulars of character, context, and teaching—accompanied by exhibits such as specific lesson plans and students' work—are integral to each case.

3. The events portrayed in these narratives are intentionally linked to teacher performance standards developed by the INTASC. The standards are cross-referenced in a chart at the beginning of the book and correspond to several discussion questions attached to each case. For easy reference, the linkage of specific questions with standards is depicted in a chart immediately following the discussion questions for each case.

HOW THESE CASES CAME ABOUT

Case subjects were selected based on recommendations from their peers and other prominent educators in reform contexts. The cases are not intended to be "models" of standards-based practice but rather to provide windows into the provocative pedagogical issues imbedded in the standards. They are examples of real practice.

Our commitment as case authors has been to report accurately rather than to endorse specific approaches to change. During the observation and interviewing, we encouraged teachers to discuss their experiences and important insights. Questions were open-ended, and we spent much time clarifying the meaning of what we saw and heard. The development process was collaborative throughout, with a mutual commitment to authenticity. In five of the seven cases, we use the real names and contexts of the teachers involved. Each principal character made his or her own decision about anonymity and authenticated the case events and descriptive accounts. As a group, the case subjects have given countless hours to be observed, interviewed, and videotaped. They were motivated by the conviction that their stories could benefit others involved in the challenges of innovation.

SUPPORT MATERIALS

Selected cases from this book as well as the earlier publication, *Secondary and Middle School Teachers in the Midst of Reform: Common Thread Cases*, are available in a CD-ROM multimedia format.

The "Instructor's Quick Guide" includes sections on "Cases as Curriculum," "Case Facilitation," and "Using Cases and Technology." Available from the publisher, it is a valuable tool for exploring the myriad possibilities for effectively promoting student inquiry, thinking, and reflection.

ACKNOWLEDGMENTS

Our collaboration on the Common Thread Case Project solidified when we realized the influence Elliot Eisner had on our quite different but complementary paths. For Traci, the first seeds of these cases were sown as Eisner's teaching assistant at Stanford. In that context she developed a commitment to qualitative research that focused on very rich and detailed descriptions of pedagogy. For Joan, Eisner's influence evolved during her study of film theory and design with Geri Gay at Cornell's Interactive Multimedia Group, where she focused her research on the complexities of narrative and visual modes of representation. Many of the research and aesthetic directions taken in this project were the result of Eisner's enduring influence, which has grown with time.

We wish to thank the many individuals who contributed to the Common Thread Cases. Those who have given valuable feedback include Sharon Brennan, Deneese Jones, Frank Mazur, Sandra Wilkins, Rita Moore, Teresa Unseld, Deborah Trumbull, Connie Bridge, Linda Hargan, Linda Levstik, and Peter Denner. Our thanks also go to Don Ingwerson for his inspirational leadership while serving as superintendent of schools in Louisville, Kentucky.

Our former graduate students provided valuable assistance at various stages of the case development process. They are Susan Brodie, Heidi Lane, Tiffini Jones, and Catherine Murray. We thank Stefanie Brimacomb, Gretchen Hill Howell, and Kathleen Miller for their diligent proofreading and constant good humor.

Videographer and digitizer Dave Vantreese captured the photographs in Case 3. Our graphic designer and multimedia specialist, Nita Kaufman, has been our compass throughout this voyage.

Consultants to the project enriched it with years of accumulated wisdom about case writing and teaching. Cynthia Ingols, a professor at Simmons College and a former director of case research at the Harvard Business School, and Judy Buzzell, associate professor at Southern Connecticut State University and author of two casebooks, provided invaluable advice and assistance. Judith Kleinfeld, professor of psychology and director of the Northern Studies Program at the University of Alaska, is well known as a pioneer in case development and research. Her continuous mentoring has seen this work from conception to fruition.

We would also like to thank those who reviewed this book for their helpful comments and suggestions: Judith Buzzell, Southern Connecticut University; Sandra L. DiGiamo, University of Scranton; Mary Lynn Hamilton, University of Kansas; Kenneth Howey, Ohio State University; J. Gary Knowles, Ontario Institute for Studies in Education for the University of Toronto; Stephen Lafer, University of Nevada–Reno; Debra Bayles Martin, San Diego State University; Betty Jo Simmons, Longwood College; and Elizabeth Simons, Kansas State University.

Our deepest gratitude goes to those teachers who have so generously opened their lives and classrooms for others to share and to Debbie Stollenwerk, our editor, whose vision parallels our own.

ABOUT THE AUTHORS

Traci Bliss, Ph.D., is an associate professor of curriculum studies and teacher education at Idaho State University. Since 1993 she has been a state policy advisor to the National Board for Professional Teaching Standards and directs the Idaho Classrooms of Accomplished Teachers project sponsored by the J. A. & Kathryn Albertson Foundation.

Joan Mazur is an associate professor of instructional design and technology at the University of Kentucky. Her research interests center on human–computer interactions and the integration of technology in various educational contexts.

John Buzzard works in marketing at the University of Kentucky Medical Center. As the project's administrative assistant, he contributed to the many facets of producing and copy editing the original drafts of this book.

CONTRIBUTORS

Jennifer Bell is an assistive technology specialist and directs a federally funded Assistive Technology Project at the University of Kentucky.

A. Edward Blackhurst is Professor Emeritus in the Department of Special Education and Rehabilitation Counseling at the University of Kentucky. He is past president of the Association for Special Education Technology.

Teri Brown is principal of a Northern Kentucky high school and a doctoral candidate at the University of Kentucky's Department of Administration & Supervision.

Judith B. Buzzell is an associate professor of education at Southern Connecticut State University and the author of several case books.

Gretchyn K. Furlong has taught in rural and urban elementary schools at various grade levels. She is currently a consultant to school districts in the development of specialized educational plans.

Harper Fouts Kelly has been an award-winning elementary school teacher for nine years. She currently teaches multiage primary in Anchorage, Kentucky.

Jane Clark Lindle is an associate professor in administration and supervision at the University of Kentucky. She also serves at the co-director of the University of Kentucky/University of Louisville Joint Center for the Study of Educational Policy.

Catherine M. Murray is a special education teacher in Pocatello, Idaho, and served as administrative assistant for the Common Thread Case Project.

Michael O'Donnell is a high school journalism teacher in Blackfoot, Idaho.

Brenda Overturf is a middle school language arts teacher in a suburban area of Kentucky. She has more than 20 years' experience in education.

Billie Jo Rylance is an assistant professor of special education at the University of Wisconsin at Oshkosh.

Gina Schack is an associate professor of education at the University of Louisville.

BRIEF CONTENTS

CASE 1
Stagnant Pools and Flowing Waters   1
Gretchyn K. Furlong, Harper Kelly, and Traci Bliss

CASE 2
Reading, Writing, and RAM   21
Joan Mazur

CASE 3
Caroline Never Smiles   57
Jennifer Bell, Traci Bliss, A. Edward Blackhurst, and Billie Jo Rylance

CASE 4
Arts on the Line   85
Traci Bliss with Catherine M. Murray

CASE 5
I Don't Think I Can Teach This Again   107
Judith B. Buzzell

CASE 6
On the High Wire   137
Brenda Overturf and Gina Schack

CASE 7
Compromise and Defeat: A Power Struggle at Watermill   161
Teri Brown, Traci Bliss, Jane Lindle, and Michael O'Donnell

CONTENTS

CASE 1
Stagnant Pools and Flowing Waters — 1

Gretchyn K. Furlong, Harper Kelly, and Traci Bliss

What happens when a teaching team discovers that an aspect of their classroom is antithetical to their core beliefs?

The teachers become aware that their math program does not reflect the same educational aims as their writing and reading programs. The math instruction is constrained by a stagnant grouping pattern that is incongruent with their mutual commitment to developmentally appropriate practice. Moreover, the teachers discover that the grouping pattern is marked by discrimination against mathematically talented females.

How will the teachers confront the discrepancies in grouping? What solution will work best with this multiage, primary classroom with forty-three highly heterogeneous students?

CASE 2
Reading, Writing, and RAM — 21

Joan Mazur

What prompts a highly successful teacher with 25 years experience to leave her position as a district language arts mentor? Once returned to the fourth grade classroom, Vicki Lugo decides to become a first grade teacher because of her belief in the need for a solid foundation of technology skills. Lugo confronts numerous challenges: updating her own computing skills, enlisting essential parental support, and developing a year-long curriculum that integrates technology with her literacy immersion approach.

Teaming with colleague Sharon O'Brien, Lugo's successes are not without concerns. Do positive results from using technology justify the additional time needed for effective integration? Would students' foundational computer and literacy skills continue to improve next year, or would they languish with less practice and technology integration?

CASE 3
Caroline Never Smiles   57

Jennifer Bell, Traci Bliss, A. Edward Blackhurst, and Billie Jo Rylance

Throughout her early elementary years, Caroline, a student with multiple physical disabilities, enjoys academic success in the regular education classroom. As she approaches middle school her grades start to plummet, she becomes increasingly isolated from her peers, and the assistive technology that has been specifically designed for her remains on the shelf. Some of her regular education teachers are astounded to discover how little they really understand one of her disabilities: Moebius syndrome. When Caroline's mother begins expressing her frustration over Caroline's downward spiral, several issues emerge about teachers' responsibilities for special needs students. Is it too late for Caroline to regain lost ground?

CASE 4
Arts on the Line   85

Traci Bliss with Catherine M. Murray

Patsy Cox teaches at Portland, a highly diverse urban elementary school in a state committed to systemic reform. Cox has always integrated art in her teaching without the assistance of an art teacher but in close collaboration with her colleagues. Consistent with the state reform goals, she embarks on intensive training in a new curriculum approach, Different Ways of Knowing (DWoK). Despite initial reservations, by the second year of the program Patsy is convinced of its value, which emphasizes integrating learning experiences through key themes. The principal of Portland is stunned to learn that Patsy has decided to move on and is concerned about the success of the new program.

CASE 5
I Don't Think I Can Teach This Again   107

Judith B. Buzzell

Eighth-grade teacher Leslie Jenkins faces the prospect of teaching *Adventures of Huckleberry Finn* with trepidation. Although she has taught it for the past two years, Twain's classic has recently come under fire in her state. African-American parents in the nearby urban district condemned the novel for its use of the word "nigger." The superintendent in that district subsequently removed the book from the eighth-grade curriculum, citing racial tension and potential damage to students' self-esteem. Moreover, many teachers admit that the book's context, dialogue, and sophisticated satire can be difficult for young students to comprehend.

Leslie is aware that although the book has stirred controversy and censorship many times since its publication, it is generally acknowledged as one of the great American novels.

How, Leslie wonders, can she prepare her class of "average" ability students to understand this classic literary work? Is she sufficiently prepared to deal with the controversial issues that may emerge?

CASE 6
On the High Wire   137

Brenda Overturf and Gina Schack

A team of middle-school teachers with diverse levels of experience designs an interdisciplinary, student-centered unit based on the teaching philosophy of a prominent researcher. The unit allows students the freedom to explore ideas and issues that concern them within the broad topic of transitions.

The students react positively to the unit and demonstrate increased motivation and fewer behavioral problems. Although the teachers are pleased with their students' performance, several voice their concerns with the student-centered teaching approach. How can teachers allow students to shape the content and progression of a unit and still be sure that certain concepts are being covered? What are appropriate assessments in a student-centered curriculum?

CASE 7
Compromise and Defeat: A Power Struggle at Watermill   161

Teri Brown, Traci Bliss, Jane Lindle, and Michael O'Donnell

Watermill Middle School was notorious for its extensive discipline problems. In an effort to improve the school, the district hired Jack Carnes, an enthusiastic administrator determined to make significant changes as the new principal. He helps to radically change the curriculum and instructional practices at Watermill and earns a statewide reputation as a successful, reform–mandated administrator.

Watermill had an active School-Based Decision Making Council before Carnes became principal. On the surface, Carnes adopts the council's procedures, but many council members believe Carnes has subverted the council's power by making independent decisions concerning new faculty hires and school restructuring.

How can teacher and parent representatives' diffuse Carnes' power, especially since he is held in high esteem by the community and throughout the state? What recourse do teacher and parent representatives have to ensure their voices are really heard? Are their expectations realistic?

Glossary   173

ISSUES MATRIX

Common Thread Cases

Issues	Case 1 Stagnant Pools and Flowing Waters	Case 2 Reading, Writing, and RAM	Case 3 Caroline Never Smiles	Case 4 Arts on the Line	Case 5 I Don't Think I Can Teach This Again	Case 6 On the High Wire	Case 7 Compromise and Defeat: A Power Struggle at Watermill
Activity/experience-based instruction							
Administration	•	•					•
Assessment	•	•	•	•	•	•	
Block scheduling					•	•	•
Collegiality issues		•	•	•	•	•	•
Critical thinking	•			•			
Curriculum sequencing		•					
Developmentally appropriate practices	•	•					
Diversity	•	•	•	•	•	•	
Heterogeneous grouping	•	•	•				
Individualizing instruction	•	•	•				
Inquiry				•	•	•	
Integrated curriculum/ interdisciplinary instruction	•					•	
Learning environment	•	•	•			•	
Multiple intelligences	•			•			•

xviii

Common Thread Cases

Issues	Case 1 Stagnant Pools and Flowing Waters	Case 2 Reading, Writing, and RAM	Case 3 Caroline Never Smiles	Case 4 Arts on the Line	Case 5 I Don't Think I Can Teach This Again	Case 6 On the High Wire	Case 7 Compromise and Defeat: A Power Struggle at Watermill
Parent involvement	•						•
Portfolios	•	•					
Professional development	•	•		•	•		•
Reflective practitioner	•	•	•	•	•	•	
Restructuring	•					•	•
Rural	•		•	•	•		
School-based decision making	•						
Small group/cooperative learning	•	•			•	•	
Student motivation		•	•	•	•	•	
Students with special needs	•		•				
Suburban		•			•	•	•
Team teaching/collaboration	•	•		•		•	
Thematic teaching				• •		•	
Urban				•			
Writing process	•	•					

INTASC STANDARDS MATRIX

Common Thread Cases

INTASC Principles	Case 1 Stagnant Pools and Flowing Waters	Case 2 Reading, Writing, and RAM	Case 3 Caroline Never Smiles	Case 4 Arts on the Line	Case 5 I Don't Think I Can Teach This Again	Case 6 On the High Wire	Case 7 Compromise and Defeat: A Power Struggle at Watermill
Principle 1 The teacher understands the concepts, tools of inquiry, and the structures of the discipline(s) he or she teaches and can create learning experiences that make these aspects of subject matter meaningful for students.	•						
Principle 2 The teacher understands how children learn and develop, and can provide learning opportunities that support their intellectual, social, and personal development.	•	•			•	•	
Principle 3 The teacher understands how students differ in their approaches to learning and creates instructional opportunities that are adapted to diverse learners.	•	•	•	•	•		
Principle 4 The teacher understands and uses a variety of instructional strategies to encourage students' development of critical thinking, problem solving, and performance skills.				•	•		
Principle 5 The teacher uses an understanding of individual and group motivation and behavior to create a learning environment that encourages positive social interaction, active engagement in learning, and self-motivation.		•	•			•	•

| | Common Thread Cases ||||||||
INTASC Principles	Case 1 Stagnant Pools and Flowing Waters	Case 2 Reading, Writing, and RAM	Case 3 Caroline Never Smiles	Case 4 Arts on the Line	Case 5 I Don't Think I Can Teach This Again	Case 6 On the High Wire	Case 7 Compromise and Defeat: A Power Struggle at Watermill
Principle 6 The teacher uses knowledge of effective verbal, nonverbal, and media communication techniques to foster active inquiry, collaboration, and supportive instruction in the classroom.							•
Principle 7 The teacher plans instruction based upon knowledge of subject matter, students, the community, and curriculum goals.		•	•		•	•	
Principle 8 The teacher understands and uses formal and informal assessment strategies to evaluate and ensure the continuous intellectual, social, and physical development of the learner.	•			•		•	
Principle 9 The teacher is a reflective practitioner who continually evaluates the effects of his/her choices and actions on others (students, parents, and other professionals in the learning community) and who actively seeks out opportunities to grow professionally.	•			•	•	•	
Principle 10 The teacher fosters relationships with school colleagues, parents, and agencies in the larger community to support learning and well-being.	•						•

CASE ONE

Stagnant Pools and Flowing Waters

THE SQUEAKY WHEEL GETS GREASED

While monitoring the groups' projects in our primary classroom, I caught Gretchyn's eye as we watched Shellie wait for the others in her group to finish a math project. She rested her chin on her hands and watched David, who was attempting to add 4 + 4.

"OK, I've got four in my head," he said haltingly as he raised his hand before him, "and I put four fingers up—one, two, three, four . . . four! 4 + 4 equals 4!"

With a sigh, Shellie agreed to help David, who was still stuck at the beginning of the project. Her math story problem adding 8 + 8 was written, drawn, and already colored, as was Theresa's. Theresa looked at Shellie and shrugged. "I know what you mean," she said.

Shellie's experience was of particular interest since during a recent transition between activities we had overheard another group member, Chelsea, stomp her foot and exclaim, "All we do is unify cubes and bears!"

The girls' comments stuck with us—and uncomfortably so. We had recently moved two boys, Robbie and Tommy, from the "Younger" ("Y") group to the "Older" ("O"), more advanced group for a variety of reasons, including their discontent with the rate of group progress. We were becoming increasingly uneasy with the idea that we may have shown favoritism to the two boys and overlooked the needs of the three girls. For the most part, Shellie, Theresa, and Chelsea sat politely and participated at the appropriate times in the "Y" group, while the two boys, when they finished their work early, would huff or announce loudly that they needed something else to do. Moreover, the three girls were effective partners for the students who did not catch on quickly. After considering the issue, we realized that it was not in the girls' best interest to move them up to the "O" group. Although they were indeed too advanced for the "Y" group, they did not yet have the skill level of the "O" students. We believed there was no other option but to leave them in the "Y" group. The underlying problem on stagnant groups in math was just too big an issue to tackle in mid-year.

Her math story written, drawn, and colored, Shellie waits in frustration as the boys in her group work through their problems.

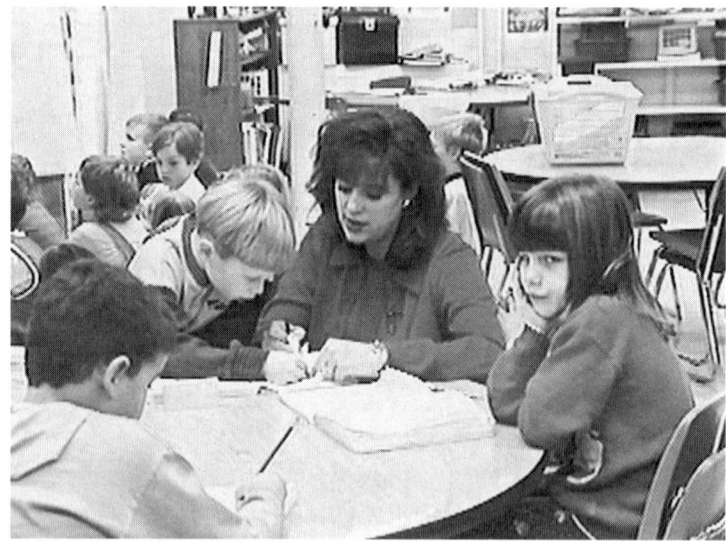

THE SCHOOL

Our school, Southside Primary, was built nearly thirty years ago. It stands alone—some might say isolated—in a historic section of Shelbyville, Kentucky, just across the tracks and about two blocks from downtown. Like the other two city schools, the facility reflects its age. Attempts to update the building's appearance have been minimal, focusing on the outward appearance (e.g., repainting or retiling) rather than basic structural needs. Individual classrooms are not only small but also noisy because of the lack of sound barriers such as acoustical tile ceilings or carpeting. The one structural change supporting statewide reform has been the installation of doors between classrooms: this promotes a cooperative atmosphere between children and teachers.

Visitors to Southside usually describe the school as inviting and child-oriented. The walls are covered with vivid student-made projects, writings, and graphs, adding warmth and vitality to each hallway. Most classroom doors are open; halls buzz with children's voices. Parent volunteers can be seen in the hallways with small groups of children, in the classrooms reading or writing with an individual child, or in the resource room preparing materials for the teachers. There is little turnover among our colleagues at Southside. While some teachers have been here as few as four years, a number of others have taught exclusively at Southside for almost thirty years.

During the first year of its inception, the School-Based Decision-Making (SBDM) council voted to adopt the multi-age classroom model for Southside. This model, originally mandated in Kentucky, consisted of grouping first through third grades together. Two years later, the council voted to change the name of Southside Elementary School to Southside Primary School, reflecting its commitment to multi-age classrooms.

Because the principal has instilled a sense of professional freedom in the faculty, teachers eagerly experiment with new ideas. However, despite their interest in innovation, most faculty members were not enthusiastic at first about grouping these grades together for the primary program. Some teachers were determined to stay within the one-grade setting, while others were willing to try two ages together but not three. However, despite this initial reluctance, each team has worked hard to make the program succeed within the classroom family concept. Because teachers were allowed to choose their own partners for team teaching, a genuine sense of colleagueship began to emerge. Gradually the entire faculty became more team-oriented, spending time together and sharing anecdotes that highlighted concerns and celebrated successes.

THE CLASSROOM

Before Gretchyn and I became team partners, our classroom had been used as two special education classrooms. As soon as we learned that we would be together in a primary classroom, we petitioned the SBDM to remove the wall between the two rooms to create one large classroom. Once the wall was removed, other problems with the aging room, such as pipes protruding from the ceiling, presented an opportunity for testing our creativity. One solution was to hang short paper streamers of all colors from the pipes, which made the basement-like atmosphere of the room more festive and inviting.

Because flexible grouping is such a vital component of the primary classroom, the room is currently arranged to facilitate many different groups meeting in a variety of situations. Two area carpets help divide the open space. An immense blue carpet is positioned on the right side of the room. Four horizontal red stripes help guide as many as forty-five children to find space to sit. Rarely, however, do we have a common lesson with all our students together—we found that children at these ages have a difficult time being attentive in such a big group. In front of the blue carpet is an imposing bulletin board with the words "Workshop Wizards" posted brightly at the top. The board organizes and guides us, as well as the students, through the many workshops scheduled each day. Under each workshop heading are invitations to mini-lessons, individual conference schedules, and other pertinent information.

In the far left corner of the room a smaller red carpet provides space for as many as twenty-five children to gather. The red and blue carpets are the cornerstones of our room because they allow us to teach all students simultaneously. The red and blue carpets have other functions as well. The red carpet serves as the class library; the blue carpet, bordered at one side by a sturdy wooden loft painted bright green and yellow, is a part of the Theater Center. The loft resembles an oversize bunk bed with a comfortable mattress and beanbag pillows where children can curl up to read and write. The bottom of the structure serves as the theater. In other corners of the room are the art, discovery, and technology centers (see Exhibit A).

Our classroom arrangements create a physical space where students can organize their time, work on their own interests, and move in and out of activities while being easily monitored by and immediately accessible to us at all times.

THE STUDENTS

"Diversified" describes the mix of children in our classroom. The children represent a range of ages, backgrounds, and abilities. Twenty percent of the students are African American.

The students range in age from five to ten throughout the course of the year. Depending on birthdays, some five-year-olds spend half of the day in our primary classroom after being in a traditional kindergarten classroom in the morning. Other five-year-olds, turning six in the fall, stay in our room full-time. At the other end of the spectrum are nine-year-olds in their final year of multi-age grouping. Students may also turn ten in our classroom if they need another year in the primary program to meet the required exit criteria before entering fourth grade.

Many of our students work on their family farms, often coming to school with hands stained from stripping tobacco plants. During harvest season, they frequently bring us fresh vegetables. There are also students whose parents work in local factories or urban Louisville. These parents rarely see their children during the school week owing to late-night shifts. Some students' parents who are doctors, nurses, and health administrators at the local hospital have been very involved in and supportive of school reform because of their own experiences with health care reform.

Our students also represent a wide range of learning profiles. Three students are hearing impaired. One of them can hear only in her left ear. A second is profoundly deaf as a result of meningitis; he relies on a full-time interpreter in the classroom—who also willingly "helps" all students. The third student has partial hearing, which is greatly improved with hearing aids. Five students identified as potentially gifted meet twice a month with the district's gifted teacher in our classroom. Four students identified as learning disabled work daily with the special education teacher. Twelve students receive individual and small-group tutoring within the classroom from Chapter 1 aides in reading and writing.

THE MATH GROUPING: EMERGING PROBLEMS

After Shellie's complaint of having to continually wait in math groups, we gradually accepted the fact that we were not adequately addressing individual differences in math. This was a difficult realization because individualized learning was something we had prided ourselves on in the language arts program.

We had organized our math program the same way for the past two years. We divided our students into two math groups: The "O" group who were p3's and p4's (previously second and third graders) and the "Y" group who were p2's (previously kindergartners and first graders). The grouping had seemed to work well the first year, so we continued with the same organization. During the second year, Tommy and Robbie were demonstrating the necessary skills to move into the O group. For example, in cooperative groups with the Y group, Tommy would make comments such as "Gosh, would you hurry up?" or he would build symmetrical spaceships with pattern blocks, which he finished well before the other students. Tommy's good friend Robbie was a gifted student who was fluent and accurate in his math problem solving. We both were astonished when he was able to calculate the difference between the gravity of Mars and the gravity on Earth; he was then able to communicate to this group, "That means that you would be three times lighter on Mars than you are on Earth!"

Parents' concerns also were a key issue. Gretchyn was well aware of the pressure from Robbie's mother. "She thought Robbie's math skills were too high for the Y group," Gretchyn recalled. "She would constantly tell me how bored he was in math. Because of her communication with me on this issue, I became more convinced that Robbie would benefit from being moved up." Likewise, I felt pressure from Tommy's mother, who repeatedly compared Tommy to Robbie.

Our goal has always been to serve the individual needs of our students in a multi-age, multi-ability classroom. We knew that to meet our own expectations, Tommy and Robbie should be moved up into the O math group.

AN UNRESOLVED ISSUE

We had never given much thought to moving other children to the O group. With the exception of Tommy and Robbie, children in the Y group were willing to cooperate with few complaints and seemed to be progressing at a developmentally appropriate pace. When we discussed whether to move Shellie into the O group, we decided against it. This group was working on two- and three-digit subtraction with base ten pieces. We believed this was too advanced for Shellie and that the move would most likely frustrate her. She had certainly been working hard in the Y group, and she was learning how to add double-digit numbers.

I asked Shellie's father whether his daughter had said anything at home that would lead him to think that she was unhappy with math.

He shrugged off the issue. "Shellie seems to be doing fine right where she is," he said, "and even if she is bored, she'll have to learn how to find something to do to keep herself busy." He thought it was good for her.

Moving one more child up in the middle of the year did not seem to be the answer. But what was? We decided we would figure out how to change math for the following year but knew we had no choice but to finish the current year as it was: stagnant groups for math and groups that ebbed and flowed for reading and writing.

THE FLOW OF READING AND WRITING

We were uneasy about this organization of our math program into two essentially inflexible groups. By contrast, our reading and writing programs allowed us to meet the developmental needs of each child as they occurred. As Gretchyn noted, "Our Reading and Writing Workshop fits our model of how an ideal primary classroom should work."

On a typical day, several children read and write either independently or in small groups. Other children use the computers to publish their own stories. We conduct mini-lessons in various areas around the room in groups of five. When not working with a small group, we meet with individual students as they create their writing projects.

"I just feel so good about the way our workshops are going," Gretchyn said. "Since we use very systematic anecdotal records based on observations, products, and conferences to decide what areas the students need help in, we can place them in the appropriate small group. By staying current with each child's progress, I think we're making it possible to develop all the necessary skills without anyone being labeled or held back by a permanent attachment to a particular group" (see Exhibit B).

One aspect of our assessment system that I find particularly effective is individual conferencing with students. In fact, I have mentioned to parents on several occasions, "My favorite part of the Reading and Writing Workshop is when I get a chance to have a conference with the kids. It gives me a chance to see where they really are, not where I think they are. They always lead me in new directions and opportunities for individual achievement."

Gretchyn nodded in agreement as she added, "I like the whole idea that no one child is stuck in one reading or writing group. Each kid is working at his or her own pace and skill level. When we put them into groups, they're almost always multi-age. The question is, though, why does the Reading and Writing Workshop seem to meet the developmental needs of all the children, while math commits children to fixed groups regardless of their current skill level?"

Harper Kelly and Gretchyn Furlong meet daily to exchange classroom observations and insights and to adjust instruction based on continual assessment.

REFLECTIVE WATERS

As Gretchyn and I dug deeper into this question during our summer reflective time, we discovered the component that made the Reading and Writing Workshops run so smoothly: flexible grouping strategies. Reading and writing activities are designed to create a true workshop atmosphere with the constant grouping and regrouping of students. Using a workshop structure with continuous assessment allows us to meet the needs of all our students in one classroom setting.

Before tackling the now-obvious missing component from our math program—flexible grouping—we decided to rename math time "Math Workshop". Although a change of name may seem superficial, it signified to us a change in mind-set. Once we committed to the concept, we knew we had to make it a reality. We now associated math with the many successes that had been exclusively for language arts.

The next step was to develop an approach that would make the math workshop concept feasible. While we already had some goals in mind, we had to develop strategies for reaching them. One framework I had read about in the book *How Big Is the Moon?* was "exploring math in relevant and meaningful contexts" (Baker, Semple, & Stead, 1990, p. 7).The authors of this book, primary teachers in a New Zealand multi-age classroom, helped children "choose what, how, and with whom they will explore their math topics" (p. 36). This scaffolding structure encouraged children to choose the appropriate level of challenge and movement. Students welcomed the opportunity to self-monitor. Through it they gained courage and confidence to take risks in areas where they might have previously felt reluctant.

As Gretchyn recalled, "The book demonstrated the philosophy we were attempting. Orchestrating a classroom always involves a delicate balance of risk taking, accountability, and responsibility toward the students. *How Big Is the Moon?* gave us specific strategies and examples of ways to maintain this balance within our newly created math workshop."

We also incorporated the Kentucky Early Learning Profile (KELP), which is an instrument for "documenting individual student learning, development, and growth during the primary program." KELP provided a rubric for gathering anecdotal records as well as additional structure for student conferencing (see Exhibit C). The math section provides learning descriptors and concepts (see Exhibit D). This assessment tool helped us place students into one of three specific groups of developmental needs: beginning, developmental, and independent/advanced groups. Moreover, because assessment is current and ongoing, it is never static or predetermined in what group a child will be placed.

A DAY IN THE LIFE OF MATH WORKSHOP: PROJECTS

"Let's get to the blue carpet for math!" With that call, some forty-three students scramble to take their places.

"It's project time!" a few students call out. Quickly, Gretchyn and I facilitate student generalizations about project work:

- Good projects have to serve a purpose.
- We need projects to show we know stuff in here.
- We've been thinking about good projects all year.

We then draw out the group in brainstorming "candidate project" ideas, such as these:

- How many marbles have we earned in the marble jar?
- Who has lost teeth, and how many have they lost?
- University of Louisville basketball fans versus University of Kentucky basketball fans

We query them:

- Why would that be a good project?
- How would you measure something like that?
- Will that serve a purpose like we talked about earlier?
- What purpose did you have in mind?

Some nominations from the floor find their way onto "the final list," while others are agreeably withdrawn by the students who suggested the concepts, enthusiasm having waned as a result of peers' questions.

Then the really critical process begins in the minds of the students—namely, "What's *my* topic?" and "Who is in *my* group?" Gretchyn and I are deliberately directive in this process. By the time students move to their newly designated groups, each child seems to be on track and involved with the task at hand. Gretchyn and I ensure this by checking carefully for understanding. While the focus of this workshop day is group planning, it is evident that students are eager to move ahead, voicing their desires with "Can we start collecting our data?"

The first steps of student work are critical especially because students often want to rush through this planning process. If the project group has not adequately thought through the topics they must address, the process can quickly become chaotic. We have specific questions to guide the students' work as we move from group to group, asking them in detail how their research is going to proceed. Also, when we conference with students at this time, we may ask simply, "What question are you trying to answer with your project?" In some cases, students struggle for a moment as they attempt to articulate their purpose. These first critical steps help ensure that all students thoroughly understand what they are asking before they begin collecting data (see Exhibit E).

STUDENT REFLECTIONS

When asked to compare last year's math curriculum with this year's, the students began with a dissection of the grouping patterns. They described last year's patterns as being limited to only Youngers and Olders, "except," as every group noted, "for Tommy and Robbie. They went up because they were real smart." Two students hypothesized that these two math wizards probably "got lots of extra help at home," while another added that "he could beat either one of them in football or soccer." Last year's grouping received some interesting praise such as, "We got to use more real things in math last year. Like when we were studying fractions, we used apples and crackers. Do you think we'll get to use them again?" Tommy and Robbie quickly pointed out that even when they were placed in the "O" group last year, the work still was not hard enough. No mention was made of why other students did not "move up" or the issue of gender exclusion, which we had struggled with. The impression from the students was that "age grouping" was simply the way things were done last year.

We then discussed the new grouping pattern begun this year. Every student interviewed preferred the new arrangement and the use of Youngers and Olders for base groups only. Comments such as, "I'm like a teacher on pluses and minuses because I'm really good at that," and "I get to teach how to work with strips" indicate that the occasional role of "student as teacher" was valued by the students themselves. Significantly, three of the more advanced students mentioned that they had learned something from the less advanced students.

The children also noted our apparent commitment to change. Nine students indicated that we would do math differently next year because "they always do new things for us every year."

We recorded our own responses to the students' reactions. Gretchen suggested, "There is a sense of safety within this structure. The students feel free to make occasional mistakes so they will take more risks. Obviously, they feel more confident when there is flexibility."

I was quick to agree: "All children believe they can learn better by reinforcing math concepts with other children. Of course, we need to make sure that this reinforcement is accurate and that the faster students are challenged to enhance their skill development."

CRYSTAL CLEAR AND FLOWING

We knew that the ultimate assessment of our new approach would be the individual progress of Shellie, Theresa, and Chelsea, the students who had precipitated the transformation. Throughout the year, we had kept a keen eye on whether the girls were being challenged, becoming more aggressive in talking about math, and able to work in groups appropriate to their developmental needs. I noted in the margin of my teacher record, "I have found that by writing anecdotal records, I am able to observe exactly what the children are demonstrating—not what I think they can do. Therefore, the children are being placed in groups that are much more appropriate than before."

In her written comments, Gretchyn noted, "If you take one child and follow him or her through the year, you will find that he or she has been in a multitude of math groupings. For example, Shellie has been in the Independent/Expanded group for the past week during our exploration of fractions. However, she was in the Developing group to help her progress in understanding subtraction facts. Once we noticed her subtraction concepts were developing quickly, we moved her and two other children into the Independent group in the middle of the week. We noted that this flexibility helped all of our students to develop more efficient strategies in learning basic facts they didn't have yet."

Flexible grouping was now working in math with the same kind of success we'd seen in language arts. Parents noticed the differences as well. At a parent conference, I asked Shellie's father what he thought of our new approach and how he thought Shellie was doing in math this year compared with last. He was amazed at the enthusiasm she was showing at home. He commented, "One day she couldn't wait to show me how she could find fractions all over the house." She now really enjoys math, even though the program is harder!

This is not the end of our change in strategies. We must continue to explore the best ways to group and regroup students based on individual needs. We realize that next year's students will bring a whole new set of needs to the learning environment. By continually assessing each student and by reflecting on our approach, we know new challenges will emerge. The key for us will be to be sure our teaching is developmentally appropriate and to offer equitable opportunities for all in our classroom.

REFERENCES AND SELECTED BIBLIOGRAPHY

Adams, T. L. (1998). Alternate assessment in elementary school mathematics. *Childhood Education*, 74(4), 220–224.

Anderson, R. (1993). The return of the nongraded classroom. *Principal*, 72(3), 9–12.

Bailey, S. M. (1993). The current status of gender equity research in American Schools. *Educational Psychologist*, 28, 321–339.

Baker, D., Semple, C., & Stead, T. (1990). *How Big Is The Moon?* Portsmouth, NH: Heinemann.

Burns, M. (1992). *About teaching mathematics*: A K–8 resource. Iowa City, IA: Math Solutions Publications.

Dever, M., Zila, R., & Manzano, N. (1994). Multiage classrooms; a new way to learn math. *Principal*, 73(4), 22–26.

Grossman, H., & Grossman, S. H. (1994). *Gender issues in education*. Boston: Allyn & Bacon.

Jeanroy, D. (1996). The results of multi-age grouping: An elementary principal documents the outcomes of meeting students' developmental needs. *School Administrator*, 43(1), 18–19.

Linn, M. C., & Hyde, J. S. (1989). Gender, mathematics and science. *Educational Researcher*, 18, 17–27.

Micklo, S. J. (1997). Math portfolios in the primary grades. *Childhood Education*, 73(4), 194–199.

Mills, C. J., Ablard, K. E., & Stumph, H. (1993). Gender differences in academically talented young students' mathematical reasoning: Patterns across age and subskills. *Journal of Educational Psychology*, 85, 340–346.

Richardson, K., & Salkeld, R. (1995). Transforming mathematics curriculum. In S. Bredekamp & T. Rosegrant (Eds.), *Reaching potentials: Transforming early childhood curriculum and assessment*. Vol. 2 (pp. 178–192). Washington, DC: National Association for the Education of Young Children.

Slavin, R. (1982). Student teams and comparisons among equals: Effects on academic performance and student attitude. *Journal of Education Psychology*, 70, 532–538.

Slavin, R. (1982). *Cooperative learning; student teams: What research says to the teacher*. ERIC Document Reproduction Service No. ED 294-926. Washington, DC: National Education Association.

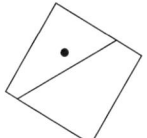

EXHIBIT A

Floor Plan of Classroom

This floor plan shows the activity centers in Harper Kelly and Gretchyn Furlong's multi-age, multi-ability primary classroom.

EXHIBIT B

Excerpts from Teachers' Anecdotal Records

PHILLIP

Math

8/21

Coming up to me: saying "I forgot how to count" but when asked "How many is this?" he said "30." "How did you know?" "I counted." Worked one on one, w/ 10 strips, counting by ones. Picked up a clock twice while working with strips. Counted by 10s with prompt.

9/15

4 – 2 = 6. Put up two groups of 4, then took away 2 fingers = 6! I put down one group of 4, he took away 2, then said "2—Oh!"

9/23

Phillip was able to write the math sentence 8 – 3 = 5 by himself when I held up the manipulative picture.

10/28

Shaded in the number 32 when asked to shade in 24. We worked on 32 yesterday.

10/30

Had drawn many ways to show 10, but only one way to show 24. "24 adding 8 equals 32." Circled 12 twos to make 24. Wrote 2 + 2 twelve times.

10/31

Very easy to talk to about math! Counted "20" 5s in the whole math. How many are in 24? Counted "1, 2, 3, 4. And one 4!" Wrote 5 + 5 + 5 + 5 + 4 = 24.
Tried to count by 5s. 5, 10, 20, 40. Do you know how to count by 5s? "No"

11/3

Excellent at counting, can go up to these: 13 + 6 = 19, 25 + 3 = 28, 36 + 2 = 38, 59 + 6 = 65. Finally too hard: 78 + 12

11/11

Can count by 10s, 5s with some trouble. Counts by 25s with help. Counts mixtures with help.

Writing

9/12

Sat right down & began writing. Some sight words evident: toys, with, bat. Many inventive spellings, but phonetically correct: Days = Daz. Some words w/out vowels: hm (him).

10/24

Phillip is working on putting periods where his voice stops.

10/26

Writing about another story he had read. . . . We brainstorm an original story. Shows lots of capitals. Will go back and fix.

11/9

Wrote I PLAYD tic tac toh. it was fun. Mini-lesson: capitals—when i stands alone, or after period, went back and fixed his own piece.

SAMANTHA

Math

8/29

Figured out how 5 is an odd number. "Because if you break it in the middle, it's not even on both sides. You have to break in half."

8/30

Smiled and raised her hand during greater than/less than lesson. Put hand down when another name was called.

9/15

"We're doing 382 – 2 and the answer is 380. I counted all this up 10, 20, 30, 40, 50, 60 through 190, um, 1,000,000? 191, 192, 193, 194 through 199, um?" I told her 200, she went 210, 220 through 290, 300, 310, through 380.

9/22

83 − 37 (estimated 15). "I'm stuck 'cause I can't take 7 away from 3 units. Can I trade a strip in for 10 units?"

10/6

Made a pattern to fill in the rhombus.

10/28

When writing what she knew about the number 24: square root of 100 + 4 = 24. Explain this to me. "That's the sq. root of 100 and that's 10 + 10 + 4 = 24!" Using circles of 3 to find how many 3s are in 24.

Writing

10/22

Samantha's troubleshooter skills on the computer are very good!

10/23

Samantha and Laura's finished product was almost perfect. They left out only one word, and they showed they understood the dialogue concepts I explained.

10/24

Wanted to read a story to me just to tell "what I like." But some ideas are jumbled and needs some organizing—organize with color codes.

11/16

Uses voice in her writing! Mini-lesson—has a long list w/out commas.

EXHIBIT C

Overview of Kentucky Early Learning Profile (KELP), 1995

Susan Brodie[1]

The Kentucky Early Learning Profile (KELP) is an instrument for primary school teachers to document individual student learning, development, and growth during the primary program. KELP was designed to help teachers monitor the progress of students in meeting the primary program objectives as established in the Kentucky Education Reform Act. KELP encourages teachers to communicate student progress to parents as well as facilitate staff development programs that focus on curriculum, instruction, and authentic assessment. The goal of KELP is to help teachers understand and document individual student development through observation and communication with parents so that curriculum and instruction can meet the needs of each student.

The Kentucky Early Learning Profile is an evolving document that begins when a student enters kindergarten or first grade and terminates at the end of third grade. During the primary years, teachers document the student's development through conversations with the student and parents, a diary of observations in the classroom, performances demonstrating knowledge, learning description summaries, and progress reports. When a student makes the transition into fourth grade, the student's KELP file is passed on to the fourth grade teacher as an important resource on the child's development and achievements during the primary years.

---

[1] Susan Brodie teaches high school in Alton, Indiana.

EXHIBIT D

Sample Lesson Plan—Fall

Learner Goal
KELP Math Component: Number Concepts

Materials
Various math manipulatives placed in a tub:

tile	money jars
bears	clocks
unfix cubes	calculators
base 10 pieces	centi-cubes
fraction bars	story boxes

Activity
The children will meet together in their family group (multi-age, multi-ability, p2–p4). The teacher writes the symbol for addition on a chart. The children and teacher engage in a discussion about vocabulary used for that symbol (addition, plus, sum, etc.). Children then share their previous knowledge of how you can "do" and "show" addition on the chart. Afterward, the students work in their journals to develop different ways to show addition.

Grouping
Students may choose to work independently, with a partner, or in a small group.

Assessment
Anecdotal records on individuals' discoveries and quotes will be used to place the children into Investigations (or skills) groups the following week. These skills may be on building the concept (or idea) of addition with one- or two-digit numbers, using manipulatives, or moving to symbolic addition up to four digits.

EXHIBIT E

Excerpts from a Student's Notes

Samantha

2/23

Question:	I wonder if it's true that people the same height jump the same distance?
Teacher:	What are going to do?
Student:	See if they jump the same height, then publish the data.
Teacher:	How are you going to do it?
Student:	(1) Measure people, (2) have them jump.
Teacher:	What resources will you need?
Student:	Measurements, standing broad jump.

3/2

Research: I wonder if it's true that people the same height jump the same distance.

Summary of research by Samantha's group

Height Matches	Distance Jumped
Ben, Rob	Ben 5', Rob 5' 9"
Mallory, Powell	Mallory 4', Powell 4'
Ben, Billy	Ben 5' 3", Billy 4' 8"
Laura, Alesha	Laura 4' 3", Alesha 4' 7"
Powell, Pamella	Powell 4', Pamella 4' 11"
Kristie, Laura	Kristie 3' 3", Laura 4' 3"

3/3

Samantha's Reflection

My question was if people the same height jump the same distance. I learned that people the same height don't jump the same distance. First, we planned out our data. Then we collected our data by measuring people in pairs that were the same height and had them jump and we found our hypothesis was wrong. We published in our math journals instead of a chart. Therefore, your height doesn't matter but it's how far you jump. Like in basketball, ice skating, ballet, track and swimming. So I learned your height doesn't matter.

DISCUSSION QUESTIONS

1. Describe the group of students Gretchyn and Harper teach. Is the group typical or atypical of most elementary classrooms? Describe these teachers in terms of their teaching philosophy.
2. Describe the physical setting of the classroom. Are underlying education philosophies evident from the physical setting alone? Based on your educational philosophies, how do you envision your classroom setting?
3. Gretchyn and Harper have used two very different types of grouping patterns. Discuss the pros and cons of each.
4. The students in this classroom represent a range of ages, backgrounds, and abilities. The underlying philosophy is that all students can learn at high levels. Explain your position on this issue. If you had a class similar to Gretchyn and Harper's, what kinds of instructional strategies would you consider most efficient?
5. In what ways did Gretchyn and Harper exhibit bias in their classroom? What other types of gender bias have you observed in elementary classrooms? What are some specific actions you could take to provide equal learning opportunities for both genders in various aspects of educational curricula?
6. Gretchyn and Harper refer to their children as "Youngers" and "Olders". How does this affect their classroom atmosphere and how the children view themselves and their classmates? What are some alternatives to placing students in these classifications?
7. The mothers of Tommy and Robbie both assertively expressed their concerns to Gretchyn and Harper about their sons' boredom in the Y math group. Pressure from these parents was an important factor in moving Robbie and Tommy to the O math group. What positive and negative impacts can parental pressure have on teachers and students? What alternative courses of action could the teachers have used in dealing with parents, including Shellie's father?
8. Gretchyn and Harper believe that flexible grouping strategies enabled the Math Workshop to become more developmentally appropriate. Discuss pros and cons of Gretchyn and Harper's approach to assessment.
9. Review the exhibits labeled "Sample Lesson Plan—Fall" (Exhibit D) and "Excerpts from a Student's Notes" (Exhibit E). These exhibits come directly from the Family Math portion of Gretchyn and Harper's Math Workshop. Imagine you are teaching the class described in this case. Divide the students into Beginning, Developing, and Independent math groups. Using the KELP rubrics and the student samples, focus on what the students can do. Finally, develop a Beginning, Developing, and Independent math lesson for each of the groups to be used during Investigations. Discuss the rationale for your strategies and activities.
10. Shellie is now part of a math program in which she can progress at her own rate. What evidence do we have that the new system of grouping is better than the previous one? What evidence is needed to make a clear determination?
11. Gretchyn and Harper orchestrated change in the classroom based on their own philosophies and practices. What are the core components of Gretchyn and Harper's philosophy? What component stimulated the change?

12. How would you rate Gretchyn and Harper's effectiveness as a team? What attributes are necessary for team teaching to be successful?
13. Gretchyn and Harper recognized a problem midyear and used considerable time the following summer to develop a solution. How effective is this approach to reflective practice? What are some alternative approaches to reflective practice?

CASE 1

Discussion Question	Corresponding INTASC Principle
3	**4** The teacher understands and uses a variety of instructional strategies to encourage students' development of critical thinking, problem solving, and performance skills.
4, 5	**3** The teacher understands how students differ in their approaches to learning and creates instructional opportunities that are adapted to diverse learners.
7, 12	**10** The teacher fosters relationships with school colleagues, parents, and agencies in the larger community to support learning and well-being.
8, 10	**2** The teacher understands how children learn and develop, and can provide learning opportunities that support their intellectual, social, and personal development.
9	**8** The teacher understands and uses formal and informal assessment strategies to evaluate and ensure the continuous intellectual, social, and physical development of the learner.
13	**9** The teacher is a reflective practitioner who continually evaluates the effects of his/her choices and actions on others (students, parents, and other professionals in the learning community) and who actively seeks out opportunities to grow professionally.

CASE TWO

Reading, Writing, and RAM

STARTING OUT

"If only I'd known what to do with them. I was a total amateur. I'd hardly ever used a computer, let alone tried to incorporate one into my classroom!"

Fourth-grade teacher Vicki Lugo had been eager to transfer to Solana Santa Fe (SSF), a new elementary school in the large urban-adjacent district of Solana Beach, in San Diego County bordering the Pacific Ocean. The diverse student population and the new high-tech facility offered challenges that Lugo sought to energize her teaching. Also, she was eager to work with principal Marge Copp, a former colleague whose skills she'd come to respect. The school was finished in late July, barely a month before the students would arrive. Lugo confronted her first hurdle as soon as she unlocked the door of her new classroom: a networked computer station and printer hummed quietly next to her desk.

In addition to the computer station for herself, three more computers arrived soon after the start of school, a donation from a parent whose company was upgrading its systems. Although she'd had little computer training herself, Lugo was convinced that elementary students needed both language and computer literacy to succeed in our technological society. The donations pushed the issue, and Lugo knew she must capitalize on the opportunity. Still, Lugo found herself with twenty-six students, some valuable equipment, and no plan for technology integration.

Enlisting the help of Janet Golden, the school's technology lab teacher, Lugo worked nights and weekends to get her skills up to speed. By mid-year Lugo had developed a range of strategies for integrating technology. "Every technology skill must have a curriculum connection" became her slogan. As the first year progressed, Lugo saw her goals take shape through a fourth-grade language arts curriculum infused with technology applications and linked to literacy skills. Using rubrics from a continuous assessment reading program as guidelines, Lugo required students to spend more than half an hour each day using the computer to work on reading or writing proficiencies.

The central program was Kid Works (www.mwcdrom.com), an integrated software package containing a word processing program, a spreadsheet, and a database. Lugo developed an on-line pen-pal program, called Key Pals (see Exhibit A). In Key Pals, students used E-mail to communicate with students in other schools who were reading the same books or gathering data on cooperative projects. Students in different schools discussed commonly read books and met literacy goals such as discovering themes, identifying with characters in a story, and offering evidence for generalizations. The district's Internet policy required parental permission, which was easily obtained since district security measures prevented students from accessing objectionable materials. Because all parents agreed to let their children participate, monitoring student access was not a problem (see Exhibit B). It didn't take long for Lugo to be convinced that her many hours of planning were justified.

"The results kept me going, especially the successes with average students," she said. "So often we spend so much time with high or low achievers. The computers make it possible to individualize instruction, but, more important, the kids are self-motivated. . . . They keep learning on their own. Once kids got their computer skills certificate from Janet Golden, their confidence soared. They helped other students and were invaluable resources to the teachers."

Spurred by their accomplishments and the principal's whole-hearted support, Lugo and Golden also designed "Tech Camp" for Solana Santa Fe's summer enrichment program. Tech Camp offered students a variety of integrated activities to build technology skills. For example, students could use a HyperCard stack for book reports. Opportunities also existed for students to use a digital camera or scanner to explore alternate ways to represent information. For $225, students attended Tech Camp daily for two weeks; scholarships were available for those students who were eligible for free or reduced-price lunch during the school year. Initially developed for fourth, fifth, and sixth grades, Tech Camp was so successful that parents demanded a similar program for children in the primary grades.

A BREAK FROM THE CLASSROOM: THE DISTRICT LANGUAGE ARTS MENTOR

Lugo's success did not go unnoticed, and she was appointed the district mentor teacher for language arts. She was in demand at all of Solana's five schools for her expertise in literacy and technology. Lugo spent her days racing between schools and tutoring teachers in computer applications. However, after her second year, Lugo returned to the fourth-grade classroom.

"I realized I could make more money tutoring students after school and still have time left for a life," she said. "I loved solving problems and working with teachers who were excited about using technology and integrating language arts, but it was just too much of a grind."

Working with young children again, she focused on eliminating obstacles to learning through the use of technology. Fourth graders did not have the necessary keyboarding skills, and Lugo felt she was spending too much time teaching basic computing. Also, she'd complained to the principal that too many of her students now came in with below-grade-level reading and writing skills. This situation was unacceptable, especially in a district with the resources of Solana Santa Fe.

OUTMANEUVERED: MARGE COPP'S PROPOSAL

A few months after Lugo's return to her fourth-grade classroom, first-grade teacher Sharon O'Brien came to Lugo for moral support. The principal, Marge Copp, was pressuring O'Brien to apply for a federal Title VII grant to provide intervention for minority students and also to train as a Reading Recovery teacher for the first grade. O'Brien was interested but didn't want the administrative responsibilities. "I'm still excited about working with the first grade," she told Lugo. "You've got to come with me to see Marge. You know how much I want to learn Reading Recovery, but don't let me get hoodwinked into doing this." Lugo understood. She had been impressed by the Reading Recovery results discussed at conferences she'd attended over the years. Like O'Brien, she had wanted for some time to be prepared in Reading Recovery but had not had the opportunity, and she was well aware of the time required to administer a grant. O'Brien scheduled an appointment, and they met with Copp the following week.

Marge's proposition was designed to appeal to the professional interests of both teachers and their liking for collaboration. They could team teach the first grade. In the morning, Lugo would have most of the students while O'Brien would pull out the Reading Recovery students for intensive literacy development. In the afternoons, O'Brien would teach math to all the children, and Lugo would administer the Title VII grants and provide technology professional development for other teachers. The following year they would switch roles: Lugo would learn Reading Recovery, and O'Brien would teach language arts and manage the considerable documentation required for the grant. Lugo and O'Brien exchanged glances and perplexed looks. They were intrigued by the possibilities. Lugo spoke first: "This gives us a whole new angle to consider." Copp gave them a week to decide.

"Marge outmaneuvered us," Lugo said after they had agreed to Copp's proposal. "She gave us an opportunity to team; we could both accomplish our long-term professional goals to become trained in Reading Recovery—all with the flexibility to integrate technology with the academic skills our students so badly needed. But I was worried. Could I take what I'd learned about integrating technology in the fourth grade and make it work in the first grade? Would it be too confusing to teach technical skills along with literacy development? How could we manage to do it all?"

VICKI LUGO

Vicki Lugo is a dynamo whose ebullience is energizing and compelling to colleagues, parents, and students alike. Her twenty-five years of experience have coalesced into a "can-do" attitude. She approaches any project confidently, no matter how daunting.

"I've been at this a long time," Lugo says enthusiastically, "and things will always work out one way or another!" Her dedication to raising student achievement is characterized by an openness to change and to new techniques. Her initial use of computers was spurred by the potential to increase individual participation and develop independence in learners—two goals that have become increasingly important to Lugo.

Lugo grew to value diversity and productivity during her own elementary school years in the 1950s. Through eighth grade, the 21 students in Lugo's class were a self-contained community at the only school in a small rural farming community in the Sacramento delta. As an Anglo-American, Lugo was in the minority of a class consisting of Filipino, Chinese, Japanese, and African American students. She remembers teachers emphasizing student performance in every aspect of the curriculum.

"We were always working on individual and group performances, and they were topics that engaged us—in social studies for example, we'd make huge topographical maps of other countries. The expectation to demonstrate what we knew was not limited to academic subjects. Before any student could graduate, she or he had to show the ability to read music and also pass a basic swimming test. After all, we lived on the Sacramento River!"

At Santa Catalina High School, Lugo developed interests in diversity and Spanish. As a junior in college she attended a university in Mexico City, where she met her future husband. They later agreed that their two children would have dual citizenship. "Over the years, we've almost always had a Mexican exchange student living with us. It has been great for our family, and it has helped us to stay bilingual, which is so valuable in my teaching."

As a result of her own educational experiences, Lugo has always believed that students must have authentic materials. In teaching her students to read, she uses a variety of books rather than basal readers. O'Brien, Lugo's partner in the first-grade experiment, credits Lugo for broadening her own teaching methods. When O'Brien started at SSF, she'd been using standard workbooks and seatwork for seven years. O'Brien was "wowed" by Lugo's holistic philosophy and her skill at integrating literature, field experiences, and art projects into language arts.

"I was stunned," she said. "Vicki's room was brimming over with books, art projects from field trips, and displays of students' written work. . . . I'd never seen students producing so much, reading so much, or enjoying themselves so thoroughly. I was scared to let go of my structured workbooks, but Vicki quickly convinced me that students could learn immense amounts on their own with proper guidance, monitoring, and structured activity."

Lugo's teaching style has been characterized by one parent as a "refreshingly no-nonsense approach" to teaching literacy. In fact, Lugo is convinced that her current approach exemplifies good teaching. She believes that teachers are largely evaluated on what she calls "canned" lessons that look good to official observers and "fluff" activities that hook kids—neither of which contribute substantially to their learning. Lugo adamantly refuses to hand in five-step lesson plans before her biannual evaluation. "I've told them, 'Come to my classroom for the morning, and after I'm done we can discuss what happened. We will focus on how I monitored students and adjusted activities to correct problems or moved students forward who were achieving their goals.' This is the heart of teaching—constantly adjusting the curriculum so students are always succeeding."

THE COMMUNITY AND THE SCHOOL

Suburban Solana Beach, north of San Diego, is a community with about 2,300 students in five elementary schools. Here, as in many border communities, one sees dramatic contrasts in lifestyle in the various socioeconomic strata.

Before Solana Santa Fe opened in 1993, a community task force (composed of parents, teachers, and professors from the nearby state university) explored how best to meet the needs of what would be a highly diverse student body. Despite controversy, the committee decided the school would offer Second Language Acquisition via an English Immersion Program rather than the district's current Transitional Bilingual Program. The majority of the committee members were convinced that for students to achieve, they needed to be fluent in English. To promote communicative goals for all students, Spanish as a second language would also be offered. Teachers who embraced these approaches were encouraged to apply to the new school as transfers. O'Brien and Lugo, both bilingual, jumped at the opportunity to teach at SSF.

Solana Santa Fe is a modern, single-story school for grades K–6. The vestibule is vibrantly decorated with a seashore motif. Starfish, shells, and seaweed are interspersed with displays of student work from a tide pool exploration project. At the center of the display, a computer station's monitor repeats an attractive screen that invites visitors to use the CD-ROM program on the tidal ecosystem.

Marge Copp, the school's first principal, chose technology, parental involvement, and diversity as themes for her new school.

"Few principals can build the school community from the ground up as the physical plant is being constructed," she said. "I felt I had a golden opportunity to shape a school that is truly a community . . . a place where everyone has access to a highly technological learning environment. I insisted the school have the wiring infrastructure to support high-speed computing, even if the computers were not initially available. I wanted that foundation and capacity from the beginning."

Despite her goals, Copp's vision was often blurred by the realities of school life. Although her plans included extensive on-site professional development for teachers in technology, faculty interest was lukewarm. "I'm not actively resisting the computers," said a veteran teacher who transferred to SSF because of her interest in working more closely with parents. "It's just that I can't find the time." Also, despite the guiding principles of diversity and community, the school has no Hispanic faculty members (although half, like Lugo, are bilingual). Furthermore, common planning time is not built into the schedule.

The faculty members relish the opportunity to share ideas with one another. One teacher, experienced but new to the school, said, "At my old school I was the star, but here everyone works together, and all are superstars. I just blend in with the crowd." The tight-knit faculty credits the team spirit in part to a five-day retreat that Copp scheduled before the school opened. It was expensive, and no other new school has been given the opportunity.

Copp's emphasis on parental involvement means parents are expected to monitor children's work at home and become active in the school community. For example, beginning in first grade, parents may be required to read with their children each night or to work with them on math activities such as counting change and writing numbers. Parents also are strongly urged to participate in orientation and support activities, such as the following:

- *Orientation*: A two-day workshop during which parents learn how to contact teachers and how to ask questions about their child's progress
- *Support*: Two workshops for parents to participate in the "Rolling Readers" program, in which they listen to their children read books daily; numerous counseling and tutoring programs available through parent request or teacher referral
- *Communication*: A Web site (http://www.sbsd.sdcoe.k12.ca.us); a districtwide newsletter; bilingual teachers; a telephone in every room for home–school communication

To accommodate Hispanic parents and further encourage involvement, informational fliers are bilingual, and instructional materials, such as books on tape, are available in Spanish. Through techniques such as the tapes, parents can help SSF achieve its curriculum goals. Teachers regularly design innovative classroom units, and there is general acceptance of new approaches. Lugo benefited from this atmosphere of teamwork, innovation, and support as she embarked on the design of her integrated technology curriculum.

DESIGNING THE FIRST-GRADE TECHNOLOGY CURRICULUM

Lugo's decision to move to first grade occurred quite unexpectedly at the end of her fourth year at SSF. Thus, she did not attend the two in-service workshops on the integrated software program for first graders. She would have to tackle the appropriate programs on her own. After heading the Tech Camp that summer, she had only one month to learn the programs, review the curriculum CDs and other on-line materials, and plan the year.

Lugo knew that creating an environment in which students could produce quality papers and illustrated texts had been key to her fourth graders' successes, but first grade was different. First graders might have limited computer experience and she could expect only emergent literacy skills. Could she design a motivating curriculum that targeted their needs? She also faced another problem: Half of the incoming first graders had been introduced to a computer and some on-line drawing tools in kindergarten, but the other half had not.

Lugo began by identifying each student's literacy skills using the *Accelerating Literacy®* developmental reading stages (see Exhibit C). Skill development is incorporated into math, science, social studies, and literature experiences. For Lugo, students would demonstrate dimensions of early literacy through several skills, such as listening to and enjoying a range of stories and books, expressing curiosity about the use of writing in communication and reading words in context, attending to modeling of story structure, and predicting story events. As the year progressed, students would use CD-ROM informational materials and other subject-area instructional software with the goal of producing several written works. Activities included writing and constructing different versions of stories. She would use two computer programs, Kid Works (www.mwcdrom.com) and Kid Pix (www.broderbund.com) to match these skills with activities. Also, based on her experience with unprepared fourth graders, Lugo insisted on teaching correct keyboarding skills from the outset, using a self-paced keyboarding program geared for young children, Mavis Beacon Teaches Typing for Kids (www.mindscape.com).

Lugo knew first graders needed repetitive tasks, but these had to be highly motivating. The correct mixture of exploration and structure was required to capitalize on children's natural curiosity while building their skills. Fourth graders could be shown the programs or skills once and then take off on their own, but first graders need continual monitoring and support to learn. Parent helpers in technology would be essential.

Finally, after working nonstop for all of August, Lugo finished her yearlong technology plan. The goal was for students to use technology as a tool for daily learning. Ten objectives defined the skills students would acquire throughout the year; each month was carefully planned to meet the objectives incrementally (see Exhibit D). Lugo agonized over the completed plan: Would it work? Would such young children lacking fine-motor skills actually be able to learn keyboarding and use the programs independently? Would they use the computer to represent various aspects of their work as the fourth graders had done so easily? Could she get the needed parent support? Also, Copp, whose vision had launched the new school and who had set the teaming plan in motion, had taken a position as the district curriculum supervisor. In the midst of one of the bigger transitions in her professional life, Lugo could no longer rely on Copp's expertise when problems arose.

ROOM 4: THE FIRST-GRADE LEARNING ENVIRONMENT

Lugo and O'Brien share the first-grade classroom that easily accommodates twenty-six students. Seven computer stations are arranged around the perimeter of a 10-foot by 12-foot alcove adjoining the main room. The computers are networked to a printer in the classroom and are also linked to the Internet via the school's wide-area network (WAN). Additional technological resources can be found in both the Media/Library Center and the computer lab. The lab's fifteen stations, additional software and CD-ROMs, and full-time instructor made it possible to increase students' access to on-line resources and individualized assistance.

Lugo's students use their classroom computers for most of their work. Parents were kept informed via a bilingual newsletter and phone calls to ensure they understood the rationale behind the extensive computer work. Lugo determined she would need six parents to assist daily in the computer area and recruited volunteers during the second week of school at "Back to School" night. She prefers parents who have relatively few computer skills.

Computer hardware, features, and functions

Computer Hardware	Source of Equipment	Computer Features	Function for Students
2 Macintosh Performas	School district	Color monitor, 16-MB RAM, sound cards and recording microphone	Create text documents, create graphics, record and play sound
5 Macintosh Performas	Parent donations	Same as above	Same as above
Apple color ink jet printer	School district	Networked color printer	Same as laser printer, but color. Can print from any computer
Internet modem connection and LAN	School district	Dial-up Internet access, dedicated phone line for school	Communicate with students in other schools via E-mail

"The best volunteers are those with no experience," she said. "I tell parents they need to smile and have lots of patience; that is the initial requirement. It's an opportunity for parents to learn these computing skills, and this keeps them motivated. I keep the parents just a small bit ahead of the children, so they can stay confident. Once they realize that they don't have to know everything and that the children often know as much or more than they do about the computers, they're fine. It's a big step for parents."

Karen Hedlund, a computer volunteer, believes she has learned as much as the students about technology.

"We're all learning so much from Vicki," she said. "I was really nervous at first, but now, if I'm stuck helping a child, I just ask if anyone knows how to help. . . . We work together. . . . The kids are just as responsible for getting the work done as we are. It really makes students proud to solve a problem an adult can't figure out."

Lugo notes that the secret to engaging parents lies in the tasks the teacher selects and assigns to the volunteers. "Volunteers need a job that matters to the children's learning—then they are committed. I'd love to give them the routine tasks like setting up stations or correcting papers, but that won't keep them coming back, and it certainly won't interest them while they are here."

Ellen Martin, each of whose three children have had Lugo in the past three years, agrees. "I love volunteering," she said. "The time I put in frees up Vicki and Sharon to spend time with the children on new skills and specific problems. I check up on the daily 'Read to Me' assignments, I encourage the children to read, help them sound out words, and work on meaning by pointing out pictures or other contextual clues. If someone is struggling, I report problems to Vicki, so she can work with students one-on-one."

Lugo began the year with basic computing skills: turning on the computer, keyboarding, and accessing programs. She posted instructions for children and parent volunteers (see Exhibit E). When introducing a new program, she taught it to the children in small groups. With each child seated at a computer, she talked him or her through it, going slowly and checking to make sure all were following. The first graders needed and enjoyed repeated opportunities to try program options such as opening or saving a file. "Learning a new program can take a week of half-hour sessions at the computer," Lugo said, "but after the continuous repetitions and examples, students take over—they rarely forget how to use the programs." However, a parent volunteer works in the computer alcove every day to provide whatever assistance the children may need.

Students spend a minimum of thirty minutes each day using a computer to refine silent and oral reading skills as well as writing. Social studies and science CD-ROMs are integrated into the language arts curriculum. Also, on many days during the afternoon math program, O'Brien uses computer programs such as Math Blaster or the Kid Pix "stamps" feature, in which students group graphics of plants or animals into exciting patterns, and meanwhile develop their spatial intelligence.

Lugo does not play down the challenges of integrating technology. "Computers can be a hassle for a teacher," she said. "There are equipment failures and mechanical problems. It can take several minutes to discover that the computer is not working because the plug is loose in the outlet."

She emphasizes, though, that the results have justified the additional time. Features of the programs, such as drawing tools, can help students see concepts and develop skills in powerful and creative ways.

"Students are completely engaged, actually doing the work," Lugo said. "They read and write and research topics for much longer than I could get them to do without the computers. They like the control and are so proud of their work on the computer. Especially in first grade—it's *legible*. That's usually a real problem, and others can read it too. We have a wall with their written computer work posted. They often arrive early to gaze and point out their own papers and read 'the wall', which displays others' work."

Teaching with Technology

Lugo claims the technology that is part of her daily lesson plans has been instrumental in formulating her current teaching philosophy.

"The use of the computers has totally changed the way I see my students and how I teach," she said. "I'm guiding them rather than directing. They learn so much on their own. I used to plan out each activity for them, step by step. Now I structure the activity so they can take those steps on their own, find their own way. Students will ask questions—if they know it is okay and expected. It's so much more meaningful. But it can be risky.

"The key to my new approach is to constantly monitor students. If I see someone staring at the computer, I go over and see if he or she is stuck and needing some attention. The beauty of the individualized instruction the computers provide is that while others are highly engaged, I have time to spend with students one-on-one. For

The key to Vicki Lugo's approach to integrating technology and literacy activities is to constantly monitor students.

example, I can be freed up to read aloud with one particular child each day rather than the usual twice a week."

Twenty percent of Lugo's twenty-six students are Spanish-speaking children. Some of their families move frequently. Often families with several children share a residence with relatives. According to Lugo, these extended immigrant families tend to be stable, with half of the mothers at home. Others of Lugo's class live in large homes in Solana Beach and have a low percentage of working mothers. Although these upscale families provide many opportunities for their children, parents are often absent, and the children are frequently in the care of nannies. Thus, the majority of these first graders are eager for attention and look to adults at school for consistent structure, encouragement, and motivation. Lugo observed that computers make it possible to teach intensive yet individualized foundational skills that require the active participation of all students.

"I think we're doing too much fluff in the younger grades," Lugo said. "I'm not opposed to fun, but it needs to be purposeful. Students need intensive reading and math work. After all, if they aren't on level for reading, they are going nowhere in this highly competitive district. A teacher can spend forty-five minutes cutting out construction paper or writing a worksheet to plan for an experience that only lasts ten minutes, must be initiated by the teacher, and has questionable learning value for students. On the other hand, a teacher can spend twenty minutes of planning time creating a lesson so that students can read or write independently on the computer for up to thirty minutes with a cognitively challenging language activity."

Lugo believes that developing skill-proficient first-grade learners is her main job. She reflected back to the days when she used a more structured basal approach.

"When I did basal reading programs, we were supposed to teach children 185 skills! At mid-year I checked my records. Were we even close to the 70-some odd skills in which each student was supposed to be proficient? With that system, we were always focused on what kids didn't know, not what they did."

Now Lugo reports that continuous assessment—a key to keeping students moving along the literacy continuum—is a manageable task. The Kid Works program is a vital assessment tool because it keeps a progressive data log of each student's work in an ongoing portfolio (see Exhibit F).

A TYPICAL DAY: GETTING DOWN TO BUSINESS

When Lugo and O'Brien's first graders come flooding into the classroom at 8:15, Lugo has already been there for an hour supervising the fourth-, fifth-, and sixth-grade Hispanic students who use her classroom computers for the federally funded math/science computer enrichment program she administers for the school.

Each day begins with the same routine, which Lugo believes is essential to good management. Students put their belongings in their cubby slots, exchange their "Read to Me" book (taken home every night to read with their parents) for a new take-home book, and sit down at their assigned round tables to review the day's activity plan. Although the content changes, students rotate daily through the following six areas:

- Journal or free write
- Desk work: brainstorming or group critiques
- Silent reading
- Read aloud to a parent volunteer to check comprehension of the previous night's "Read to Me"
- Spelling work
- Computer work

Beginning at 8:45, groups composed of various skill levels rotate through the stations in half-hour intervals until the 10:30 recess. Following recess, the rotations continue from 11 to 12:30. During this time students meet with O'Brien for Reading Recovery,[1] or they work individually with Lugo as needed. Each day, Lugo systematically assesses progress by kid watching and keeping anecdotal records as they work alone or in groups.

As students in the computer rotation take their seats in the alcove, Lugo and a parent volunteer check the students' handwritten materials for typing into the computer. Instructions for the day's work are briefly clarified and students begin. For example, during the first month of school, students worked on their first computer assignment, a self-portrait. First they filled in the blanks on a hard-copy handout: "My name is _____; I like to _____." They then typed this into the computer with hands placed correctly on the keyboard. Finally, students used the draw program to sketch a self-portrait. As the year progresses, the assignments become more cognitively challenging. Student progress is assessed using the *Accelerating Literacy®* Model (see Exhibit C).

In this classroom, technology helps solve motivation problems associated with practical aspects of literacy achievement. Lugo uses the classroom computers to

---

[1] Fifty percent of the Reading Recovery students are Spanish speakers who receive instruction in alphabet recognition and sight words.

combine the needed skill repetitions, which otherwise could become tedious or boring, with tasks that maintain students' interest. The kids can use color graphics or variable font sizes to keep their focus on words and meaning. "They love it," Lugo reports. "Students can type the word BIG then increase the font size so that BIG appears on the screen." The computer work provides the critical practice time students need to work on individual skills.

For example, one ESL student, Emmelyne, had severe inattention and low literacy skills. Additionally, she did not qualify for Reading Recovery because her skills were just slightly higher than the cutoff. As soon as Lugo observed that she was beginning to match pictures to initial sounds and catching on to the rereading strategy, Emmelyne was rewarded with additional computer time to add clip-art pictures to her writing (see Exhibit F). Motivated to practice, Emmelyne's incentive to write words that matched the illustrations she'd inserted had a significant effect. Lugo recorded a marked increase in her vocabulary on her *Accelerating Literacy®* Reading Portfolio.

Uriel, a shy Hispanic boy who spoke virtually no English initially, worked with O'Brien each day in Reading Recovery. He had trouble remembering vocabulary, and his writing skills were poor. Uriel worked for long periods of time on modeled writing prompts such as fill-in-the-blank stories. Lugo's anecdotal records showed that Uriel remembered vocabulary from the modeled writing prompts he'd put on the computer (see Exhibit F), and he was given additional time in the alcove. The on-screen display seemed to provide the reinforcement he needed to visualize sentence patterns and remember words in context. Lugo and parent volunteers coordinated their efforts to closely monitor and reinforce his vocabulary and comprehension skills.

Matt, an advanced reader, seemed to be able to read any material he was given. Placed immediately in the most accelerated of the six reading groups, he remained there throughout the year. However, Lugo observed two issues concerning Matt's

Emmelyne shows her enthusiasm for using the computer to illustrate her writing.

skills: (1) he lacked creativity and had difficulty comprehending and summarizing all he had read; (2) he often became bored and constantly needed new, stimulating work to stay engaged. Using a program called Storybook Weaver (www.broderbund.com), Lugo was able to spark Matt's creativity. The program uses dramatic graphic backgrounds and an assortment of fantasy characters that can be cut and pasted together to form creative story lines. To keep Matt engaged, Lugo assigned him additional computer work related to a language arts–math project. He used the database program in Kid Works to compile the statistics on students' favorite foods as part of a unit on data collection, description, and representation (Exhibit F). By the end of the year, Emmelyne, Uriel, and Matt were at grade level for all skills. Lugo noted how these very different students prospered: "The technology enabled me to use multiple paths to literacy for getting through to these kids—each with a very different problem." Though she felt confident that Matt and Emmelyne would be successful in second grade, she worried Uriel might backslide without constant follow-up and support.

These students' successes demonstrate Lugo's belief that it is critical to teach to students' individual learning styles and provide computer materials that allow students to explore their linguistic, mathematical, or artistic talents.

"At the computer, each child can manipulate text, play with shapes and draw pictures, select illustrations, or listen to sounds that heighten their attention to language forms and vocabulary. It is an intense experience that goes hand in hand with the other immersion activities that are part of my approach. Students have to *think* about writing, reading, and hearing language, and with the computer it's easy, fun, and they can show what they know."

TECHOSAURUS

By May, Emmelyne, Uriel, Matt, and the other first graders had completed all the work assigned for the year. As a reward, students could request a topic of their choice. They chose dinosaurs. Lugo's four-week unit served as a capstone for the year's literacy and technology work.

The room decorations and displays were changed. The wall-mounted papier-mâché tide pool from a previous unit was transformed into a prehistoric landscape, and dinosaurs appeared amidst the crepe paper vegetation.

The Dinosaur Unit used all the language arts activities and regular stations with which the students had become familiar. The children learned about dinosaur characteristics, their ecosystems, and their habitats through dinosaur sticker stories and free writes on dinosaur facts. They learned songs and poems about dinosaurs, made a class mural showing the three periods of dinosaurs, and used an interactive CD-ROM program "Learning about Dinosaurs."

The culminating activity of the Dinosaur Unit required students to invent a dinosaur and list its characteristics, the period in which it lived, and its environment—including food sources and natural predators. Using the draw tools in Kid Works, students sketched the imaginary dinosaur and its habitat and then transferred the project to the Kid Pix program, where it could be presented as a slide show.

Lugo confessed her amazement at the children's progress and ability to produce the illustrated texts on the computer. "I have friends who can't yet use word processing and draw programs to accomplish what these six- and seven-year-olds have done," she said. "We have to check continually to make sure they are using correct keyboarding, but essentially there were no skills planned that they did not learn. And they have been so creative!"

High expectations were the critical element. Lugo believes that if she and O'Brien had limited the possibilities for students or not insisted they read, write, and use the computers daily, the students' achievements would have been quite different.

A COLLEGIAL DILEMMA

Lugo and O'Brien began debriefing on the year's experiment in mid-May. Although both felt an enormous sense of achievement and professional growth, each had a serious concern. Lugo was worried about the continuity of instruction for the first graders. Could next year's instructors maintain the technological skills her students had acquired? The second-grade teachers were using computers, but not at the intensive level of integration students had come to expect in her class. She had insisted, for example, on combining keyboarding skills with simple narrative coherence. Would both these essential skills continue to improve, or would they languish or disappear with a lack of practice and technology integration? How could she bring up this touchy subject with colleagues?

O'Brien was concerned about the following year when, according to the deal they'd struck with Marge Copp, she and Lugo would reverse roles. Lugo would handle the Reading Recovery in the morning, and O'Brien would provide the technology integration for the literacy immersion program. Could she maintain Lugo's high academic standards? Could she get up to speed with the computers? Even though she had adequate computing skills, she believed Lugo's were far superior—especially in the seamless way she managed instructional computing. Lugo was so cool with mechanical problems; she never seemed to get rattled. O'Brien planned to spend the summer polishing her skills and practicing technology lessons, but she still worried that her lack of confidence would hinder student's technological foundations.

Also, a new principal, Julie Burke, was due to arrive in August. The landscape had changed. Burke was perceived as supportive of teachers and very involved with students, but by her own admission, she didn't have the technology expertise of her predecessor, Marge Copp.

REFERENCES AND SELECTED BIBLIOGRAPHY

AskERIC *Virtual Library*. http://ericir.syreduc/Virtual. One of the leading Web site repositories of lesson plans on the Internet, contributed by teachers.

Balajthy, E. (1991, February). Keyboarding, language arts, and the elementary school child. *The Computing Teacher*, 40–43.

Banks, J. A., & Banks, C. A. (1991). *Handbook of research on multicultural education*. New York: Macmillan.

Blair, T. R., & Jones, D. L. (1998) *Preparing student teachers for pluralistic classrooms*. Boston: Allyn & Bacon.

Buckleitner, W. (Ed.). (1998, Winter). *The elementary teacher's sourcebook of children's software*. Vol. 4. Patterson, NJ: Active Learning Associates.

Cochran–Smith, M. (1991). Writing processing and writing in elementary classrooms: A critical review of related literature. *Review of Educational Research*, 61(1), 107–119.

Collaborative Ideas Web Site. www.k12.wv.us/wschool/html/lesson/collab.htm.

Cuban, L. (1986). *Teachers and machines: The classroom use of technology since the 1920s*. New York: Teachers College Press.

Delpit, L. (1995). *Other people's children: Cultural conflict in the classroom*. New York: New Press.

Robyler, M. D., Edwards, J., and Havriluk, M. A. (1997). *Integrating educational technology into teaching*. Upper Saddle River, NJ: Merrill/Prentice Hall.

Rancho Santa Fe Web site. www.sbsd.sdcoe.k12.ca.us

Tatum, B. (1997). *"Why are all the Black children sitting together in the cafeteria?" and other conversations on race*. New York: Basic Books.

EXHIBIT A

Key Pals Project

Vicki used the Key Pals project in the fourth grade for reading critiques and exchanges. First-grade students used the Key Pals project in this exhibit to collect data for Matt's database project (see Exhibit F).

Class _____

Your Name _____

Key Pal's Name _____

Week 1: Sending a message
- Find your **mailbox**.
- Enter your **password**.
- Put your key pal's name in the **subject bar**.
- **Address** your message. (Whose class are you sending it to?)
- Type in the following information:

  Hi,
  My name is _____. My favorite color is _____.
  I am _____ years old.
  From,
  _____ (type your name)

- **Send** your message.

Week 2: Reading a received message and sending a reply
- Find your **mailbox**.
- Enter your **password**.
- Find your name and click twice on the paper **icon** to open your mail.
- Read your message.
- Click on **Reply**.
- Select **Memo**.
- Type in the following information:

Dear (key pal's name),
My favorite food is _____. My birthday is _____ (Date).
_____ (type your name)

- **Send** your message.

Week 3: Receiving a message/Closing/Starting a new message/Zap Shot picture

- Find your **mailbox**.
- Enter your **password**.
- Find your name and open your mail.
- Read your message.
- Close the message window.
- Select New.
- Put your key pal's name in the **subject bar.**
- **Address** your message.
- Type a message of your choice to your pal.
- **Send** the message.

Week 4: Using the info
Database: How to sort (rank) the information

The following info can be determined for each of the participating classes or just the "home" class. The info has been defined by class so that it can be used for additional projects if desired.

Class _____

What was the favorite color? _____ (#?) _____

What was the favorite food? _____ (#?) _____

What month has the most birthdays in it? _____ (#?) _____

What is the most common age? _____ (#?) _____

Week 5: Viewing our key pal pictures
- Have computers at Advanced or Super User level so the desktop is available.
- Gain access to the appropriate **server** for the home base of the key pal.
- Double click on the Server icon to open the menu.
- Go to the Zap Shot folder where photos are stored.
- Open the folder for your key pal's class.
- Double click on the photo **icon** and "Meet your Pal".

Week 6: Using the info (Continued)
Option 1: Pictographs
Using a draw program, students can create columns and then stamp in appropriate visual responses to the data. They will have to determine the names of the columns and what they are trying to demonstrate. This can be very structured or open ended depending on the class and the amount of "charting" experience they already have. See the following example.

Favorite colors in Vicki Lugo's class

Green	Blue	Red

Option 2: Venn Diagram
A Venn diagram can be used to show which students have things in common. Each student should have a blank Venn diagram chart, a class list, access to the database, and a pair of scissors. Looking at the data, the students can place the info in the appropriate space.

EXHIBIT B

Parental Permission Form for School Internet Use

Solana Santa Fe, like most schools, requires parental permission for any student use of the Internet. The following form was developed to address concerns about the appropriateness of materials used and supervision of students using the Internet.[1]

SOLANA BEACH SCHOOL DISTRICT
Acceptable Use of Internet and Information Systems Contract

We are pleased to offer students, faculty and staff of Solana Beach School District access to the district computer network for electronic mail, the Internet and other information systems. This access is limited and is subject to District policies, rules, regulations, and restrictions, as they may be adopted and amended from time to time. This use is also subject to all applicable laws.

No student will be granted access without written consent of the student's parent or guardian. That consent can only be given by signing and returning this contract to the District. PLEASE READ THIS DOCUMENT CAREFULLY BECAUSE IT WILL BE A BINDING CONTRACT WHEN SIGNED.

Access to these resources through the district is a privilege, not a right. Notwithstanding any provision in this contract, the district may revoke access at any time by giving written notice to the parent or guardian.

When using the District's computer network, the student's behavior can affect the other students as well as the employees of the District and the public. A student's activities while using the network must be in support of education and research, and consistent with the educational objectives and the rules and regulations of the District. In addition, a student accessing the Internet and other information systems, using District network equipment and facilities, is responsible for all on-line activities which take place as a result of the student's access. No access is permitted without the permission of and the general supervision of an employee of the District. IMPROPER USE OF THE NETWORK WILL RESULT IN THE CANCELLATION OF THE STUDENT'S ACCESS PRIVILEGES AND REVOCATION OF PERMISSION TO USE THE NETWORK, AS WELL AS DISCIPLINARY ACTION BY SCHOOL OFFICIALS.

---

[1]Reprinted by permission of Solana Beach School District, Solana Beach, CA.

What is improper use is defined in district rules and regulations, which may be amended from time to time. By the way of example and illustration only, the following is a list of some of the uses which are unacceptable:

- using impolite, abusive, offensive, or otherwise objectionable language in either public or private messages;
- using the Internet or other resources for sending or retrieving confidential, illegal, obscene, or other material unrelated to the educational objective for which access is granted;
- placing on the Internet or other information systems material which is confidential, illegal, obscene, or unrelated to the educational objective for which access is granted;
- sending, receiving, copying, or changing copyrighted materials without first obtaining all required permission;
- knowingly or negligently allowing any other person to obtain the student's password;
- using another person's password;
- damaging, destroying, removing, copying, or abusing any district equipment, including but not limited to computers, modems, printers, and software.

Retain Top Portion for Your Information

- -

Return Bottom Portion to Your Child's School

Parent/Guardian's Agreement

As the parent or guardian of the student identified below, I have read and carefully considered this Contract. I have also had a full opportunity to discuss this matter with school officials and to familiarize myself with the nature and content of the Internet and other information systems available through the District network system. I understand that employees of the District may not always be able to prevent and restrict access to controversial and sensitive materials on the Internet and other information systems.

I give my consent to the District granting this access to my child. I release the District and its employees from any responsibility or liability resulting in any way from my child's use of this access privilege or based on any materials the student acquires or sees as a result of access by the student or others. I also agree to accept full responsibility for supervision and control of my child if and when my child has access to the Internet or any other information system without using any District network system or equipment. I understand that the District and its employees have no relationship to such nonschool use. I understand that I can revoke this consent only by written notice, delivered to the school administration. I understand that the District also can revoke this access at any time, upon notice to me.

*Parent/Guardian*_____*Date* _____

_____No—I will not permit my child to use Internet services.

Student's Agreement

I understand and agree to abide by the principles and guidelines of this contract.

Student's Name (please print) _____

Student's Signature _____ *Date* _____

*Teacher's Name*_____

EXHIBIT C

General Description of the *Accelerating Literacy*® Model

Accelerating Literacy®
Kindergarten through Sixth
Walker Enterprises
650 Columbia St. #415
San Diego, CA 92101   (619) 237 9836
(888) 253 5450 Fax: (619) 236 9576
www.literacy-for-all.com
Evaluator: Dr. Rena Walker

General Description

The *Accelerating Literacy*® (AL) Model provides teachers with the base of knowledge they need to teach reading and writing preschool through sixth grade. The AL Model meets the needs of all students, including those who are bilingual, considered to be at-risk, gifted, or have special needs. Data collection procedures, data analysis, instruction, critical thinking, assessment benchmarks, and students' literacy development are articulated across the grades. *Accelerating Literacy*® emphasizes balance in three areas: Curriculum (math, social studies, literature, science); literacy (read-aloud, shared reading, guided process reading, silent sustained reading, modeled writing, and guided process writing); and processing (using semantics, syntax and graphophonics to construct meaning). *Accelerating Literacy*® presents the necessary components of balanced instruction to demonstrate how district grade-level text, literature, trade books, and the basal readers are put together to form a cohesive instructional PK - 6th grade program. The AL staff development model has three components - training, implementation, and coaching. These pieces work together and provide students with effective, consistent instruction.

In Brief

Accelerating Literacy®, a preschool through sixth grade literacy model, was developed by Rena M. Walker. Introduced in southern California in 1990, AL has been successfully used in more than 1000 schools to date.

Reproduced by permission of Dr. Rena Walker, Walker Enterprises, San Diego, CA 92101. All rights reserved

Goals

The model assists teachers in establishing benchmark standards, identifying student's needs, establishing consistent instructional expectations, assessment procedures, and monitoring students' achievement across the grades. An increase in teachers' effectiveness and efficiency of instruction is evidenced within a few months of implementation. The model has been found to be effective in all types of schools, including Title I, in urban and rural settings. Participation of parents is recommended and explained through Reading Clubs and Read to Me Programs. Data analysis computer software is provided. Schools utilize their grade-level text and books/stories found in basal series, literature, and trade book collections.

Results

Students' achievement gains have been documented by participating schools. A self-monitoring system is presented in AL to provide teachers with easy access to pertinent data so they can make instructional adjustments and revisions. Teachers and administrators have consistently reported that students are more actively engaged in processing print and more motivated to read and write. Teachers improve their decision-making through analyses of student data. The initial step, analyzing and collecting baseline data, is presented in the AL Model as follows: Kindergarten and first grade students are assessed on print awareness, and listening/speaking development. Students are then staged developmentally in reading, writing, listening, and speaking. Second through sixth grade students are initially placed in reading through information gained from oral reading records and comprehension assessments. A Reading Class Profile Sheet for each class is developed (computer assisted) and used by the teacher to plan effective instruction in guided reading and components essential to balanced instruction. Each student's data is placed on reading and writing portfolios and used in parent, administrator, and teacher conferences.

EXHIBIT D

Lugo's First-Grade Technology Plan

Lugo's yearlong technology plan shows the progression of technology skills, beginning with keyboarding basics and progressing through the use of more complex programs. Students are assigned to computers and learn the basics of navigating and inputting information using Kid Works during the first two months. Additional tools and resources are then added. There are tools for generating texts and representations of information (such as Storybook Weaver and draw programs) as well as content CD-ROMs (such as the Dinosaur CD).

Technology Plan for Vicki Lugo, First-Grade, SSF

Goal
Students will use technology daily, as a tool for learning.

Objectives
1. Students will have the ability to use all fingers when typing.
2. Students will gain a knowledge of draw programs, Kid Pix and Kid Works.
3. Students will be able to manipulate font, size, and location of printed text.
4. Students will be able to write sentences and stories on Kid Works and then illustrate them. They will be able to change fonts and print their work.
5. Students will be able to use Super Print to make cards or posters.
6. Students will be able to write a story with a beginning, middle, and end on Storybook Weaver.
7. Students will be able to enjoy a Discis Book on CD-ROM.
8. Students will be able to manipulate an informational CD-ROM.
9. Students will continually work on Reading Maze (a phonics program), Word Munchers, and Jack in the Beanstalk.
10. Students will be exposed to and use two or three math software programs.

September
- Begin drawing programs.
- Begin writing.
- Begin keyboarding.

Activities

I. Assign students to computers.
II. Teach how to turn on and use At Ease.
III. Teach how to get into Kid Pix (this was learned in kindergarten) Free Exploration
IV. Teach Kid Works (see instructions, Exhibit E)
   The students write:

   My name is _____.
   I like to _____.

   Then the student does a self-portrait.

October

- Begin keyboarding on Kids Keys.
- Begin word processing; teach how to change fonts so that students begin to recognize letters written different ways.
- Continue drawing.

Activities

I. Frame sentences: A *jack-o-lantern is* _____.
II. Frame story: *This is a bat. A bat has* _____. *A bat has* _____. *A bat can* _____. *A bat can* _____.

III. Halloween poetry

   _____ *here,*
   _____ *there,*
   _____, _____,
   Everywhere!

These programs will be done in Kid Works and will be illustrated.

November

- Continue with keyboarding, emphasizing the use of all ten fingers.
- Continue to use Reading Maze and introduce CD-ROM books.

Activities

I. Fall is. . . . This is a poem done in Kid Works and illustrated with leaf rubbings.

   Fall is. . . .
   _____,
   _____,
   _____,
   and _____.

December
- Introduce Super Print.
- Continue with keyboarding.
- Introduce Word Munchers.

Activities
I. December is. . . . (done in Kid Works and illustrated).

December is a time for
_____,
_____,
_____,
and_____.

II. Students will make a Hanukkah or Christmas card using Super Print.

January
- Keyboarding for five minutes at the beginning of each computer session.
- Introduce Jack in the Beanstalk story writing in small groups.
- Introduce Storybook Weaver.
- Introduce Math Blaster—math.

Activities
I. Resolutions for the New Year (the last words of the second and last lines rhyme)

It's 1999
La, la _____,
This is the year I'll
_____!

II. Winter stories (poem done in Kid Works and illustrated)

Winter is when. . . .
_____ are _____,
_____ are _____,
_____ are _____,
and _____ are _____.

III. Descriptive writing, "*My Snowman*," with illustration

February
- Continue with keyboarding, Reading Maze, Word Munchers.
- Emphasize Storybook Weaver so that the students really begin writing stories on their own.

- Begin E-mail Key Pals; work with this in the lab and in the class.
- Use the Internet with the rain forest study.
- Math word problems on Kid Works.

Activities

I. Storybook Weaver stories
II. Have students type stories from their journals in Kid Works.
III. Students make Valentine's Day cards for their parents in Super Print.

March

- Story Writing
- Continue with Key Pals, Reading Maze, Jack in the Beanstalk, and keyboarding.

Activities

I. Rain forest stories on Storybook Weaver
II. Rain forest animal stories

   A_____ *lives in the rain forest.* (Then the student writes three sentences about the animal of choice.)

III. Database work in the lab

April

- Let students have more free choice about using the computer.
- Emphasize the use of Storybook Weaver for writing software.
- Continue with keyboarding, Reading Maze, and writing software.
- Introduce Thinker Things—math.

Activities

I. Spring vacation story writing. Given the topic sentence, "*During Spring vacation* I *did many fun things,*" the students add three to four sentences and end with "*I had a fun vacation.*" (These are not illustrated but printed on pastel-colored paper.)
II. Storybook Weaver stories about the ocean.
III. Tidepool animal stories—each student writes a story about the tide pool animal of choice. These are illustrated and done in Kid Works.

May

- Keyboarding, Storybook Weaver, and Jack in the Beanstalk
- CD-ROM used for information on dinosaurs
- Introduce Learn About Dinosaurs.
- Introduce Count Down—math.

Activities

I. Acrostic Poem—each student chooses an ocean word to go with each letter of his or her name.
II. Dinosaur stories; description and illustration of an invented dinosaur.
III. Father's Day cards in Super Print
IV. Label dinosaur pictures on Learn About Dinosaurs.

June

- Free Choice activities
- Practice using Kid Works and printing independently so students can be tutors next year.
- Use Kid Pix to produce a slide show of the creative writing dinosaur descriptions.

EXHIBIT E

Kid Works Instructions

1. Sign in.
2. Select Story Writer, write your story, and save.
3. Select Go, highlight Story Illustrator, draw, and save.
4. Select Go, highlight Story Writer, select open, and highlight the story you want to print.
5. Read your story.
6. Put the cursor at the beginning of the story and choose your picture from the picture box at the bottom of the screen.
7. Select Go, highlight Story Player.
8. Listen to your story and then print if it sounds right. If not, you need to fix it; go back to the Story Writer to edit your story. Then go to step 7.

EXHIBIT F

Samples of Student Work

Samples of student writing and representational work using computer tools are as follows:

1. Emmelyne's patterned writing poem "December Is a Time for. . . ."
2. Uriel's acrostic (also called a name poem) using ocean words to match the letters of his name.
3. Matt's database of favorite foods for Lugo's class with three representations of the data (the numeric data sheet, a Kids Stamps diagram, and a Venn diagram generated using the Kid Works word processing and draw program).

Emmelyne's illustrated December poem.

December is a time for....
Kwanzaa,
Christmas,
my family,
and lighting candles.
by Emmelyne.

Uriel's acrostic (name poem).

Urchin   Rock
Ray   Octopus
Isopod   Jelly
Eel   Abalone
Limpet   Shark

URIEL   ROJAS

Case 2

num	Class Lugo	Lugo Birth M	Class Lugo Fav C	Lugo Age	Lugo Favorite Fo	Class Hayes
01	Elyse	July 4th	green	6	Pizza	Megan
02	Brianna	Nov. 6th	green	7	Pizza	Lexi
03	San	March 15th	green	7	Pizza	Justine
04	Alexandra	Sept.	Pink	6	Pizza	Jaclyn
05	Jena	Feb 8th	blue	7	Pizza	Alexa
06	Brooke	Feb 17.	blue	7	Pizza	Karli
06b	Brooke	- -	- -	- -	- -	Seung Yeon
07	Ilana	March 20th	blue	6	Pizza	Allie
07b	Krysta		Blue	6	Pizza	Blaire
08	Chantal	Aug. 14th	blue	6	Pizza	Kenzie
09	Emmelyne	Sept. 11	pink	6	Pizza	Katie
10	Charles	March	red	7	Spaghetti	Kelli
11	Edgar	Dec.	green	7	Oranges	Vincent
12	Timothy	Feb 24	green	7	Macaroni & Cheese	Jerrud
13	Makoto	Nov. 17	green	6	Watermelon	Spencer
14	Tyler	Feb 21	red	7	Chicken Noodle Soup	Christopher
15	Garrett	June 27	blue	7	Pizza	Nathan
15b	Garrett	- -	-	- -	- -	Brandon
16	Stephen	June 19th	red	6	Pizza	James D
17	Uriel	April 19	white	6	Pizza	Eric
18	Casey	Sept. 6	green	6	Pizza	Tyler
19	Christophe	April 5th	green	6	Pizza	Alex
20	Rafael	April 12th	Red	6	Strawberries	Graeme
21	Matthew	May 19th	Red	6	Pizza	Kenneth
21b	Matthew	- -	- -	- -	- -	James R.

Database for Lugo's class.

Matt's chart of the "favorite foods" data.

pizza 10

Class Lugo Favorite Foods

by Matthew and Chris

watermelon 2   orange 1

Matt's Venn diagram of the most common class responses.

Pizza

6 years old

Blue

DISCUSSION QUESTIONS

1. What is Vicki Lugo's philosophy of teaching?
   - How did her philosophy evolve from her own educational experience?
   - How is technology integral to her philosophy?
   - How might her approach be translated into other subject areas?
   - How might her philosophy be limiting for diverse learners? For example, is the notion of independent learning (rather than collaborative learning) culturally dependent?
   - How might a teacher with a different philosophy (less holistic) use the strengths of this approach to teaching literacy?
2. Lugo notes that learning to use computers can be time-consuming and that mechanical difficulties can cause classroom implementation problems. Give examples from the case that illustrate these two potential problems. Might there be a positive side to occasional mechanical problems? What might children learn from solving technical problems themselves or observing their teachers do so?
3. Lugo devoted a great deal of time to learning to use computers. How realistic is it to expect novice teachers to expend this effort? What are other demands on their time? Which demands should take priority and why? What dictates the demands?
4. Lugo notes that one particularly strong argument for using computers in first grade is to enhance the legibility of children's handwriting. What are the advantages and disadvantages of using computers to address this problem? Consider children's fine-motor development, for example. How might the use of computers delay or enhance the development of fine-motor skills?
5. Lugo notes that teaming is a key factor in her success. She works with O'Brien and Golden and also includes parents in her "classroom instructional team."
   - What are the advantages and disadvantages of this strategy? How does this approach relate to valuing diversity? Explain.
   - How might a teacher who does not have the extensive parental and professional resources achieve similar technology/literacy integration to support instructional goals?
6. Discuss the pros and cons of the Lugo–O'Brien team.
   - Given the success of the current arrangement, should the plan for next year be modified so that the teachers don't switch roles? Weigh the apparent benefits of their professional development versus the children's apparent best interest.
7. Parental involvement is emphasized at SSF and in Lugo's classroom. Discuss the advantages and disadvantages of such extensive parental involvement.
   - In Lugo's classroom, parents participate primarily in support roles. What might be advantages and disadvantages of involving parents in the planning as well?
8. Determine whether Lugo's use of technology is developmentally appropriate.
   - How is *developmental appropriateness* defined at the early childhood level?
   - In what ways did Lugo use technology to promote (1) children's learning of information; (2) children's exploration and discovery; (3) children's learning of concepts; and (4) children's social interaction? How developmentally appropri-

ate were these? What other ways might she have used technology to enhance these areas?
- How might Lugo use computer technology to affirm the language backgrounds and cultures of nonnative English-speaking children?

9. Consider Lugo's curriculum in general.
   - How justified is her emphasis on language arts? Take into account factors such as the children's grade level, socioeconomic backgrounds, and linguistic backgrounds.
   - What other areas of the curriculum might she be sacrificing, and what potential losses exist for the children?
   - Consider Lugo's emphasis on skill development. To what extent is her approach appropriate given children's varied developmental and instructional needs? Give evidence from the case to support your position.

10. Lugo is concerned about the second-grade teachers' use and integration of technology into the curriculum.
    - In traditional areas such as mathematics, reading, and social studies, teachers carefully consider the scope and sequence of the curriculum. Should there be a scope and sequence in technology education? Explain why or why not, and if so, how might this be implemented?
    - How might Lugo address her concerns with the teaching staff? What might her role be in training teachers?

11. Lugo and O'Brien stress individualized literacy skills building. By the end of the case all of their students have met the grade-level requirements. To what extent can their success in promoting literacy be attributed to their use of technology as opposed to other aspects of their program such as Reading Recovery or extensive parental involvement?

12. Assess the various avenues that Lugo and the school provided for diverse populations. Do these opportunities adequately meet the needs of the student body?

CASE 2

Discussion Question	Corresponding INTASC Principle
5, 7	10 The teacher fosters relationships with school colleagues, parents, and agencies in the larger community to support learning and well-being
8	2 The teacher understands how children learn and develop, and can provide learning opportunities that support their intellectual, social, and personal development.
	3 The teacher understands how students differ in their approaches to learning and creates instructional opportunities that are adapted to diverse learners.
9	5 The teacher uses an understanding of individual and group motivation and behavior to create a learning environment that encourages positive social interaction, active engagement in learning, and self-motivation.
	6 The teacher uses knowledge of effective verbal, nonverbal, and media communication techniques to foster active inquiry, collaboration, and supportive instruction in the classroom.
9, 10	4 The teacher understands and uses a variety of instructional strategies to encourage students' development of critical thinking, problem solving, and performance skills.

CASE THREE

Caroline Never Smiles

Cast of Characters

Mr. Cristoff, physical disabilities resource teacher
Caroline Ellington, special education student
Kate Ellington, Caroline's mother
Ms. Johns, counselor
Ms. Shelton, Caroline's sixth-grade teacher
Ms. Ward, sixth-grade social studies teacher
Mr. Wiley, fifth-grade teacher

At the Belle Vista sixth-grade dance, heavy metal music pounded across the gym, reverberating out into the dimly lit stucco hallways. Adolescent boys milled on one side of the gym, hands in low-slung pockets and legs contorting in odd positions while the girls clustered in half circles, legs swaying casually amid muffled giggles. Only rarely that evening did a courageous suitor venture alone across the wide, newly polished gym floor to ask a classmate to dance.

Like her female classmates, Caroline had devoted much time to preparing herself for the first dance of the year—a much-anticipated occasion. Her hair, elegantly braided with a grosgrain ribbon, sparkled under the fluorescent lighting. Her new lime-green outfit was the latest in preadolescent chic. Unlike the rest of her class, however, Caroline did not participate in the circle prelims. After her mother dropped her off, Caroline entered the gym and eagerly watched her classmates, but only for a few minutes. Then, precariously perched on her prosthetic legs, she abruptly reversed her forward direction and walked out under the glaring orange exit sign. She moved slowly, winding her way down the empty hallway to the quiet isolation of the school cafeteria. She was glad to see her resource teacher, with whom she spent one period a day outside the regular classroom. After talking with him briefly, she moved to sit with a group of girls, where she remained until her mother arrived to take her home.

Caroline's masklike expression is caused by Moebius syndrome. Weak facial muscles prevent her from smiling.

PHYSICALLY SPEAKING

"Why doesn't Caroline ever smile?" asked Ms. Ward, who taught the sixth-grade social studies class to which Caroline had been assigned. "You know, she seems like such an unhappy child."

The members of the Individual Education Plan (IEP) team who were gathered to discuss Caroline Ellington's transition from elementary to middle school turned to the girl's mother, Kate Ellington, and awaited her response. The answer came loud and clear. "Caroline *can't* smile like you and me."

This simple explanation caught Ward and the other educators off guard. They glanced around at one another, each hoping someone else would be the first to speak. "I wanted to crawl under the table after I asked the question," Ward later recalled. Although school had been in session more than a month, the teachers at Belle Vista Middle School were unaware of the full nature of Caroline's disabilities. Ellington's explanation answered the teacher's question, but none of the teachers fully understood the parameters of the rare genetic disorder, Moebius syndrome.[1]

---

[1] The Moebius Syndrome Foundation provides information at P.O. Box 993, Larchmont, NY 10538; phone (914) 834-6008.

Moebius syndrome, identifiable at birth by a masklike expression, is readily apparent, especially when the child laughs or cries. Facial weakness, muscle paralysis, or defective development of the jaw and tongue also causes difficulties in speech and swallowing. Other physical abnormalities accompanying the disorder may include clubfeet, dislocated hips, and more or fewer than five digits on the hands and feet.

For Caroline, Moebius syndrome has affected her ability both to show facial expression and to speak. Although her communication skills have far surpassed the expectations of medical and clinical experts, her partially paralyzed tongue gives her voice little volume and causes articulation problems. Consequently, her speech is difficult to understand, especially for inexperienced people trying to communicate with her for the first time.

In addition to the Moebius syndrome, Caroline was born with other physical abnormalities. Her left arm ends just below the elbow joint, and her legs terminate just above the knee. She uses prosthetic legs to move short distances and switches to an electric wheelchair for longer ones. When not wearing her artificial legs or traveling in her wheelchair, she ambulates her body by using her right arm in a crutchlike manner, lifting and swinging her body forward for each "step." She uses her foreshortened left arm to support and pivot her movements, a technique she taught herself during early childhood (see Exhibit A).

Surgery was used to ameliorate other physical problems such as creating an appropriate closure in her trachea. However, the stoma[2] still opens slightly when Caroline coughs or clears her throat, causing air to enter the trachea. When there is cool weather or the wind is blowing, Caroline can't be outside because she feels as though she can't breathe.

Caroline has beautiful translucent skin, a very slender build, fine features, and a chestnut brown ponytail. Sitting in her wheelchair, her right arm rests gracefully on the chair's arm. When she speaks, she often uses her arm to gesture and emphasize a point.

Caroline lives with her parents, Kendal and Kate Ellington, in a gated, exclusive community of upper socioeconomic families in a western state. Kendal is a vice president of a well-established insurance company, and Kate is a full-time homemaker. At 13, Caroline is the youngest of three children. Kelly, who attends college, is 21, and Matt is 16. "Caroline's independence and ability to keep up with everyone else are a tribute to her family who have 'done the right things,'" remarked Caroline's elementary school speech/language pathologist (see Exhibit B).

Friends and acquaintances would describe Kate Ellington as a positive thinker, who raised Caroline to be her own best advocate—to take responsibility for her actions and to accept the consequences.

Caroline, according to her mother, exhibits all the traits of youngest child syndrome. "She is funny and loves to play the role of the comedian and practical joker. She might even be considered a rascal at times." Very independent, Caroline refuses

---

[2] An incised opening in the throat maintained for drainage after removal of a trachea tube following a tracheotomy.

to identify herself as disabled, and accommodations at home provide her as much independence as possible. For example, breakfast items, snacks, and even treats for the dog are all placed within Caroline's reach either on lower shelves in the cupboards or on the bottom racks of the refrigerator.

Kate explains how adept her daughter is at reading facial expressions, body language, and emotions. She believes that Caroline's perceptiveness leads her to give people what she thinks they expect. For example, if teachers don't expect much from Caroline, she doesn't give them much in return.

According to her own account, Caroline is happy with herself and enjoys school. Like her peers, she enjoys "complaining" about her teachers and has mood swings, particularly when it comes to relationships with parents, teachers, and other students. She experiences typical adolescent problems organizing school work, getting to class on time, maintaining good personal relationships, and wearing the "right" clothes. These normal developmental adjustments, however, are always compounded by the additional accommodations Caroline must make to cope with her disabilities. "I wish I looked like other people," she confided to a classroom aide.

THE SCHOOL DISTRICT

The Adams County School District is typical of many large consolidated urban districts located in the western states. Encompassing the city and several urban-adjacent areas, it includes 46 elementary, 12 middle, and 6 high schools. A significant portion of families have low personal incomes: one-third, or 14,000 students, qualify for free or reduced meals. The 12% of students who qualify for special education services are comparable to the national average of 10%. Caroline's middle school, Belle Vista, reflects the demographics of the immediate neighborhood—a situation quite different from the district as a whole. The majority of the students come from families in the average to above-average socioeconomic strata, and only 9% qualify for free or reduced lunches. About 18% are non-Anglo.

During the 1980s and early 1990s, national focus on educational reform prompted administrators in the district to institute major changes. Once a junior high modeled on the open classroom pod concept of the 1960s, Belle Vista is now a burgeoning middle school with a 13% overload and several portable classrooms. The flat-roofed, brick building is distinguished by the lack of windows in most classrooms. Dividing walls erected in what were once the open spaces for pod classrooms left many areas of the school with no natural lighting.

Like its regular education counterpart, the Adams County Special Education Department has been committed to reform. Special education administrators adopted a collaborative and inclusionary stand by placing students with special needs in regular classrooms across the entire school system. Special education teachers were encouraged to collaborate with regular education teachers by providing cooperative or auxiliary instruction for students with disabilities within the regular classroom.

Belle Vista, which includes grades 6 through 8, was committed to the middle school model early on and quickly moved from departmentalized instruction to a team-teaching model. Small groups of teachers work with approximately 150 students. Each team has four teachers, one for each of the basic academic classes: math, science, social studies, and reading and language arts. Using this team approach, teachers have developed an integrated and thematic curriculum. The core subjects are augmented by exploratory classes in technology, home economics, art, speech and drama, and three foreign languages.

Tensions between new practices and old methods persist, however, at Belle Vista. In spite of a district-wide policy committed to a middle school structure, and a philosophy that emphasizes holistic, integrated teaching, many teachers continue to use lecture and recitation almost exclusively. In these classrooms little emphasis is placed on peer interaction. Despite the availability of team-planning time, these teachers use only discipline-based texts and present material in a lock-step fashion, with no apparent attempt to make cross-disciplinary connections.

The school offers five special education programs. Two are resource areas for students with mild learning and behavioral problems. Three are self-contained programs: one each for students with severe behavioral disorders, learning disabilities, and physical disabilities. The middle school has a four-year record of success in educating students with physical disabilities. According to the special education teachers, it is the cooperation of the regular classroom educators that results in the successful inclusion of students with physical disabilities.

Caroline's full inclusion at Belle Vista is a continuation of the policy that began when she first enrolled in the school district. Starting with first grade, she always attended classes with students her own age in regular classrooms. But because of her pronounced physical disabilities, Caroline also received special education services based on an IEP.[3] In early grade school, the speech/language clinician worked closely with her. During all her school years, teachers especially knowledgeable about physical disabilities were available to guide and support her. Although Caroline's family could well have afforded to enroll her in a private school, one especially designed to meet the needs of students with disabilities, they chose instead to enroll her in the Adams County School District because of its emphasis on inclusion.

ACADEMICALLY SPEAKING

"Caroline seems to have shut down this year," Kate Ellington sighed as she addressed the IEP team during the meeting she had requested. "I mean she was not a straight A student in fourth and fifth grade, but she has never had D's and F's on her report cards before middle school" (see Exhibit C).

Ellington's concerns about her daughter's academic and emotional progress in school were well founded, especially given the new demands Caroline faced in middle school. However, problems were beginning to develop long before Caroline reached

---

[3] According to the mandates of PL 94-142 (the Education for All Handicapped Children Act of 1975) and PL 101-476 (Individuals with Disabilities Education Act), Caroline's main entitlements are defined as a series of rights to free and inclusive education.

Belle Vista. Caroline's eligibility for special education services had been determined by various assessments. The evaluations centered on speech-language tests, adaptive behavior scales, and achievement tests. These measures were used because her problems initially appeared to be totally physical. No IQ measure was ever administered to evaluate the possibility of cognitive delays or learning disabilities. In addition, no social-emotional evaluations were ever given.

Following speech and language assessments, Caroline received language therapy in the primary grades and benefited from these services. But they were discontinued later in grade school because extensive school and medical tests indicated that she was surpassing expectations. Given the constraints imposed by Moebius syndrome, Caroline's speech volume and enunciation were far better than leading experts predicted. Nonetheless, uninformed listeners found her hard to understand, and she was unable to project her voice beyond the immediate vicinity. After becoming accustomed to Caroline's speech patterns, most teachers reported having little difficulty understanding her.

By law, students who qualify for special education must be reevaluated every three years. Among the tests used for students with physical disabilities are adaptive behavior scales, which measure the degree of personal independence and social responsibility achieved by an individual. A recently administered scale of adaptive behavior indicated that Caroline earned scores in the "adequate range" in the areas of communication, daily living skills, and socialization. Although all her scores were reported as "adequate," interpersonal skills stood out as her greatest strength.

A series of third-grade academic achievement tests indicated that Caroline's reading and written expression were average for her age and grade. Reading comprehension posed more difficulties for Caroline than word recognition. Moreover, she scored well below the average range on tests of mathematical achievement. Both her mathematics reasoning and mathematical computation levels fell significantly below the average of age-similar peers. Her resource teachers had not concerned themselves with this area of her development and, in fact, were unaware of the test scores. Consequently, no referrals or recommendations had been made to address the problem.

Since her earliest days in public school, Caroline had attended mainstreamed classes in all academic areas. Like most elementary students, she remained primarily in one classroom taught by one teacher in each grade. Mobility posed only minor problems. When Caroline needed to move from the main classroom to specialized ones offering art, music, or computers, she used her wheelchair. During a typical school day, Caroline needed the physical assistance of an adult only to get on and off the bus and to use the bathroom.

During her first four years of elementary school, Caroline consistently received support from her peers. They helped her get materials from her backpack or desk many times throughout the day. When she needed help maneuvering her wheelchair in and out of the classroom or through the hallways, other students quickly came to her aid. According to Caroline's mother, students were eager to sign up for days and classes in which they could be Caroline's helper. Clearly, the optimum strategies of inclusion were working well in this environment.

A radical change occurred, however, in the fifth grade when Caroline's peer-helper support system abruptly ended. The school administration, afraid of a potential lawsuit that had been threatened by parents of another student with disabilities, terminated the peer support policy for all students with disabilities. Caroline felt the change immediately. Mr. Willey, her fifth-grade teacher, adhering strictly to the district memorandum, suddenly discouraged students from helping Caroline physically. At the same time, he erroneously assumed that if Caroline needed help she would now ask him. However, instead of asking for help—something Caroline was unaccustomed to—she began to withdraw and contribute less, even in her best subjects. Without the help of her classmates, it took Caroline longer to find needed materials, and she frequently dropped them. Soon she had more problems organizing her work and getting on task. Although Willey noticed that she interacted less with her classmates and spent more time alone, this issue was never discussed with Caroline's IEP team. Willey offered to help Caroline during and after school with her academic work, particularly mathematics, but this approach met with minimal success. Her parents hired a private tutor to assist Caroline in mathematics.

The transition to sixth grade and the Belle Vista Middle School's structure compounded Caroline's problems. Still lacking peer support, Caroline now had to move hourly from classroom to classroom, adding to her organizational problems. She had difficulty maneuvering her wheelchair in the school's overcrowded classrooms and bustling halls. These logistical issues meant that, for the first time in her life, Caroline was usually late for her classes.

Although she had only been at Belle Vista a short while, Mrs. Ellington became increasingly concerned about Caroline's burgeoning problems. In addition to problems with mobility and organization, her academic grades had been on a gradual but steady decline (see Exhibit C). By midterm of her first year in middle school, her grades declined to D's in most subjects, and she had failed both social studies and science.

By Halloween of the sixth grade, Caroline's falling grades became such a grave concern that her mother called a special meeting of the IEP team. The team consisted of Caroline's parents, her regular and special education teachers, and a school-based special education consultant. Caroline declined to attend; she claimed she had work to finish and the meeting was probably unimportant anyway. Revising the full-inclusion plan of the previous spring, the IEP team now recommended that Caroline spend time daily in a resource room for students with physical disabilities. For the first time in her public school career, Caroline would spend time in a special education classroom. Seemingly embarrassed, Caroline referred to this as "my study hall time."

Initially, Mr. Cristoff, the physical disabilities resource teacher, reported that Caroline's special resource class was beneficial. She regularly sought help, asked questions, and worked industriously on her assignments. But as the school year progressed, she became withdrawn and stopped requesting any instruction or assistance. Although Cristoff frequently asked whether she needed help, Caroline indicated she did not. She claimed everything was OK and that she understood her assignments. Cristoff did not check her work or confer with her regular classroom teachers but instead accepted her self-evaluation.

Another problem for Caroline was that she was significantly slower than her peers at taking tests and quizzes in her regular classroom. Because she consistently was unable to write the answers to open-ended test questions in the allotted time, her IEP team proposed another remedy: A classroom teacher or assistant would record Caroline's responses. But once again, Caroline refused help with the tests, preferring to tackle them on her own. She insisted on the independence, which she believed had been a key to achieving success during her first five grades.

Ms. Shelton, Caroline's sixth-grade language arts teacher, lent support to Caroline's quest for autonomy through a seemingly inadvertent gesture. Caroline had unexpectedly shared with the class some background on her disability (see Exhibit D) and how it might have come about. Shelton quickly responded, "Everyone has a disability, whether it is academic, physical, or social. People have to overcome their disabilities and do the best they can with what they have."

TECHNOLOGICALLY SPEAKING

One day, in the fall of Caroline's first year in middle school, after completing a language arts lesson, Shelton asked the class to begin work on a new reading assignment. Sitting at her desk, she answered individual students' questions that needed clarification or further explanation. All of a sudden, looking down, she saw Caroline on the floor beside her using her arm for balance. "How did you get here?" Shelton asked, stunned.

"I don't think she knew I was surprised," she recalled later. "I tried not to act surprised, but I thought to myself, 'How did you manage to get here?' I had never seen Caroline do that before [i.e., move about without her wheelchair] and I didn't know she could."

Caroline did not appear at Shelton's desk by accident. She had pressed the remote control switch to lower her wheelchair using the electric lift. She traveled to the front of the room by using her right arm to lift and swing her body forward for each "step."

Caroline surprised Ms. Shelton when she unexpectedly left her wheelchair and "scooted" up to retrieve a book.

After speaking to Shelton, Caroline returned to her wheelchair in the same way she had come to the front of the classroom. Using the wheelchair to raise herself back to the level of her desk, she transferred to her desk chair and continued with her assignment. "The rest of the class was not surprised that Caroline came across the floor," said Shelton. "I suspect Caroline has done this in other classes."

Indeed, from first through fifth grade, Caroline used her self-designed method to travel within the classroom. Even though the teachers, parents, and other support personnel had met at the beginning of the year to plan for Caroline's education, no one had explained Caroline's various travel modes to Shelton.

In elementary school, Caroline's self-propelled motoric techniques had served her more efficiently for short distances. During grade school, she "scooted" across the classroom floor to sharpen her pencil, get to the teacher's desk, and make presentations to the class. Because Caroline stayed in the same classroom most of the school day, this short-distance form of mobility presented few challenges.

Caroline was fitted with prosthetic legs, but she seldom used them. The artificial legs could not bend at the knee, and while she was seated, one leg extended at nearly a right angle from her body due to problems with hip alignment. In addition, the legs were heavy and awkward, and they placed a considerable amount of physical pressure on her hips and upper thighs.

During her last year of grade school, Caroline was scheduled for flexible artificial leg replacements that hinged at the knee. According to Willey, Caroline was eager for the new legs to arrive. Unfortunately, they did not live up to Caroline's expectations. First, there was difficulty with proper fit, and she developed sores on her stumps, a common occurrence with prosthetic legs. Second, the knee hinges would sometimes collapse without warning, and she would fall. The falls were embarrassing and compromised her independence. According to reports, Caroline received extensive support from her parents, the school physical therapist, and the orthotist who fitted the prosthesis, but the legs just did not meet her needs. Not surprisingly, Caroline discarded the new legs by the end of the fifth grade.

Belle Vista Middle School, and the sixth grade, presented obstacle courses that challenged Caroline's mobility. The classrooms were small and crowded, the hallways were congested and seemed more narrow, and she now had to make frequent trips to her locker. Since Caroline had already stopped using her artificial legs, and scooting was not possible for long distances, only her wheelchair remained. The wheelchair option was one she had used infrequently during elementary school, preferring instead the independence her scooting provided.

Middle school teachers tried to accommodate Caroline's wheelchair by placing it in the very back of the room. To give her extra time, she was excused early from classes so she could travel down less crowded hallways. While these modifications helped Caroline's mobility, they increased her isolation, often leaving her alone and missing some of each class. She was no longer an integral part of any class.

The school district also made efforts to support Caroline's school progress by using technology. Toward the end of fourth grade, her IEP team met to plan her fifth-grade academic program. Because Caroline had functional fingers only on her right hand, they discussed her need for assistance in working with computers. The team was in agreement that a technological device or program might help her to use a computer more efficiently. The team requested an evaluation to determine whether assistive technology (see Glossary) would be appropriate for Caroline.

In spite of the law and the intent of Caroline's IEP team, nothing was done during the summer between fourth and fifth grade to pursue support through assistive technology. In October, the IEP met again and made a formal request for a technological evaluation for Caroline. By the following June, an evaluation by an outside consultant was completed. Finally, in February of her sixth-grade year, the IEP met with an assistive technology specialist to discuss the evaluation report. The team was aware that in making decisions about the type of technology tools or supports a particular student might require, the recommended process is to start with nontechnology solutions and then work up the continuum to higher-tech solutions as needed. Although the specialist offered a range of solutions, the team recommended that the district purchase a high-technology BAT keyboard for Caroline. Easily portable, the BAT is a plain, four-by-four-inch, one-handed consolidated keyboard that works with a computer. Caroline received the BAT keyboard in late spring, a full year after the team's first request for technological assistance. Upon arrival the BAT turned out to be for the wrong computer platform (Macintosh- vs. IBM-compatible). The keyboard was exchanged, and one compatible with IBM computers finally arrived. Next, the keyboard had to be modified because it was too large for Caroline's hand. She could not access all the keys so the keyboard was sent to a rehabilitative engineer. The engineer had to fabricate a whole new system that emulated the original BAT and worked by being attached through it to the computer. Although the district hired and paid an outside consultant to provide training, there is little evidence that Caroline or her teachers were trained, and no training was provided for family members. At that point, her mother requested that she be allowed to take the keyboard home over the summer. When hooking up the keyboard caused the family computer to malfunction, it was put on the shelf. Since Caroline had always done quite well in her computer classes and had even won an award in one, neither she nor her family saw the use of the new device as a priority.

When Caroline began at Belle Vista, she left the BAT at home. Even though the computer class was her favorite, she made no mention of the device or that she had been told it would improve her speed. Prior to the beginning of the year, her resource room teacher had been told of the keyboard but had not received training in its use or been reminded of its availability. Further, even though use of the BAT keyboard was documented on the IEP, her teachers only remembered the BAT's existence when they were contacted by the public relations officer at the district office. Concurrent with a new emphasis on assistive technology for students with disabilities, a film crew was scheduled to videotape Caroline using the BAT.

Meanwhile, the assistive technology specialist claimed that, all along, he had assumed Caroline was using the BAT regularly and proficiently but simply hadn't followed up once Caroline had taken the device home.

SOCIALLY SPEAKING

Caroline's social problems surfaced in the fifth grade. One day, in tears, Caroline appeared in Ms. John's office. Caroline told the counselor that some of the girls in her class were talking about her, making fun of her, and ignoring her. She demanded something be done. As Johns probed the situation, Caroline identified what she perceived as a clique and named the girls involved. Johns acknowledged that these particular girls were known to pick on other students who looked or acted different. At the same time, the counselor thought it was unusual that the problem arose in the fifth grade. As far as she knew, Caroline had always gotten along with her peers. Since Johns was currently working with the fifth graders on developing self-esteem, Caroline asked to be allowed to take part in one of the presentations to the class. Johns suggested that Caroline share with the class some of her feelings about being disabled and how people often treated her differently.

Excited about this opportunity as well as a bit nervous, Caroline asked her mother to be part of the presentation. "I can't do this," Mrs. Ellington told her daughter. "You have to find your own words for this. I can't fight your battles."

As Caroline gave her well-rehearsed talk to the class, sharing how it felt to be excluded, she tactfully mentioned no names. But Johns noticed that some of the girls who were part of the clique seemed to lower their heads to hide their embarrassment. After Caroline finished talking to the class, she summarized her talk by playing the song *Healing*, by Wynnona and Michael English. This poignant song details how the struggle to heal eventually results in growth, strength, and finally the serenity of self-acceptance.

When the song ended, she asked the class whether they had any questions. No one raised a hand. Then, without prompting from Johns, the students applauded and raced to recess. Although Johns was originally apprehensive about Caroline's presentation, she felt the class reacted maturely to the lesson—it was a success.

That evening after supper, Caroline received a phone call from Sherri, one of the girls in the clique. Sherri said she was calling from a friend's house and wanted to apologize for her unkind behavior. Caroline discussed her subsequent attempts to build a friendship with her.

"I get home from school and this girl from my class calls. She says she wants to say she is sorry for treating me bad. I asked her if she wants to come over and play. She says no because she is going to the ice cream store with some friends. I called her the next morning, and her mom said she had left. That girl lied about not being able to come over. Nobody ever called me before, and I don't know how they got my number. They called for a trick."

Johns felt initially that Caroline's personal relationships improved after the talk. But a few months later, the girls claimed that although they were now trying to be friendly, Caroline was ignoring them. They accused her of seeking attention. The girls reported that Caroline turned her back or did not answer them when they talked to her. They interpreted Caroline's behavior as anger toward them and decided to leave her alone rather than make her more angry.

By the time Caroline reached middle school, this fifth grade social dilemma had developed into a pattern of exclusion and seclusion. Teachers reported that Caroline seldom talked with other students. She traveled alone in the hallways and sat at the back in every classroom. At the end of the school day, she was immediately helped onto the bus, excluding her from taking part in extracurricular activities. At noon, she invariably ate by herself. But no one referred Caroline for personal counseling, a school district service for which she was eligible.

Caroline did participate in class discussion when the topic broached her disabilities. After studying the book *Twenty-One Balloons* (DuBois, 1946/1986), members of Caroline's class raised questions about the results of repeated intermarriage among a limited number of families. Shelton explained the problems that sometimes resulted from these marriages, citing examples such as the genetic link between the royal families of Europe and hemophilia. She used the examples as the rationale for state laws prohibiting the marriage of close relatives.

Caroline's hand shot up the second Shelton stopped talking. Caroline explained to the class that her father had traced their family history. As a result of his genealogical research, Caroline and her family surmised that a grandmother might be responsible for her disability. After a long pause in the discussion, Shelton asked Caroline whether her grandmother felt guilty about passing on a disability. "No," responded Caroline. "Besides, I like me just the way I am."

EPILOGUE

Between Caroline's sixth and seventh grade, the Adams County School District embarked on a more focused effort to use assistive technology for children with disabilities. Newly available federal funding made this a priority. During the summer, the district's assistive technology coordinator and Caroline's special education teacher worked individually with her to better understand her needs. This effort included several conversations with Mrs. Ellington.

At about the same time, Caroline's family initiated a redesign of the prosthetic legs discarded a year earlier. As a seventh-grade student, she was now excited about her new legs. They were longer and fit better with specially added Velcro. Socks, neatly pulled over her stumps, served as a buffer to prevent pinching and make the prostheses more comfortable. While the wheelchair remained in the hallway for trips between classes, Caroline now could maneuver into and around any classroom using her new prosthetic legs. "I enjoy walking in school now," said Caroline.

At the suggestion of the resource room teacher and assistive technology coordinator, Caroline was assigned to a specific seventh-grade team—"The Tigers"—widely known as the "caring team." The team included teachers who were enthusiastically committed to integrated thematic units in math, science, English, and social studies. They also made a special effort to involve students with special needs in all team activities. They accomplished this by modifying schedules, using a detailed team behavior policy, and providing extra support for homework assignments. These strategies emphasize individual growth and accountability, which the group claimed made its behavioral referral and failure rate lower than that of other teams. In the Tiger Team classrooms, students are most often seen engaged in cooperative learning, peer conferencing, one-on-one instruction, and independent project work.

The teachers also stress good communication. Team members talk regularly with parents via phone calls, notes, and parent-teacher conferences. Teachers send daily notes home, which itemize homework assignments and evaluate the student's academic and behavioral progress. "Caroline looks forward to going to school now," Mrs. Ellington commented, adding, "She seems to be getting her work completed and is earning higher grades than last year." While Caroline's grades in seventh grade have improved overall, recent assessments indicated that Caroline might have a learning disability in math.

Caroline's progress in the social area is mixed, and thus far the possibility of counseling has not been discussed. After Thanksgiving, the Tigers went on a day-long field trip to a local science museum. At the insistence of her teachers, this was Caroline's first school trip without her mother. When the day finally arrived, she was excited about her independence but glad to have been assigned a buddy for the trip, Josh Madden. Caroline reflected on the connection with Josh. "He was like my best friend, or at least I thought he was. He talked to me a lot on the bus. But now he just says 'hi' in the cafeteria."

When asked who her best friend was, Caroline identified her classmate, Sandy, a student with multiple disabilities (e.g., cerebral palsy, cognitive delays). "We get to be together on the bus and during first period. And I got to go to her birthday party in June," exclaimed Caroline. "But we don't see each other outside of school because my house doesn't have any wheelchair ramps, and Sandy can't leave her wheelchair."

Sensitive to Caroline's lack of friendships, her parents broached the subject of a facial operation. This operation might allow Caroline to smile like other young people for the first time in her life. Having read in the national press about Chelsea Thomas, a child with Moebius syndrome whose surgery had produced a beautiful smile, Caroline's parents suggested that she might consider the same surgery. Quickly and vehemently, Caroline responded that she was not interested—that she had already been through too many operations. Caroline's family supported her decision. But Kate Ellington struggled with the implications and recalled the words of Chelsea's mother:

> Smiles are so important; they help us connect to other people, to communicate. They let people know that we're interested, that we're friendly. Being without that vital connection can be very isolating for a child. As her mother, I know Chelsea is interesting and friendly and bright. But [before the operation] the rest of the world couldn't tell, at least not at a glance.[5]

Due to a professional promotion for Mr. Ellington, the family moved to an adjacent state the following year. The faculty at Caroline's new high school make every effort to support her. Their intent is to meet her special physical needs in such a way that she can acheive academic success. "At last, someone is listening to us," Kate Ellington said.

---

[5]Thomas, L., & Stich, S. (1996, November). Our daughter couldn't smile. *Time*, 71(11), 31–34.

APPENDIX A

Special Education Mandates

A. Edward Blackhurst

Special education and related services for students are mandated by federal laws that have their roots in Public Law 94-142, which was passed by Congress in 1975. This law has been amended several times and is now known as IDEA, which is the acronym for the Individuals with Disabilities Act. IDEA guarantees the right of all children with disabilities to a free and appropriate education in the least restrictive environment. An Individualized Education Plan (IEP) must be developed for each student who has been diagnosed as having a disability. As part of the IEP planning process, parents, teachers, and administrators are required to consider the technologies that may be useful in helping a child meet the objectives in the IEP.

When special education students reach adulthood, their rights to accessible employment will be protected by PL 99-506, which amended the Rehabilitation Act of 1973 by adding Section 508 to that act. Section 508 ensures access to computers and other electronic office equipment in places of federal employment. The guidelines ensure that users with disabilities can access and use the same computer equipment and programs as other users and that modifications will be made in the work environment to facilitate employment of people with disabilities.

Two other important laws affect the way schools, governmental agencies, and businesses provide access for people with disabilities. PL 101-336, the Americans with Disabilities Act (ADA), broadened the types of agencies and employers covered by Section 508 requirements and mandated additional protections, such as accessible public transportation systems, communication systems, and access to public buildings. These requirements are opening many avenues of employment for people with disabilities who were heretofore excluded from office work because of inaccessible equipment and work environments.

Public Law 100-407, the Technology-Related Assistance for Individuals with Disabilities Act, was signed into law in 1988. Under the auspices of that act, all states are developing systems to provide a variety of technology assistance to children and adults with disabilities and their parents and guardians. The purpose of PL 100-407 is to provide financial assistance to states to enable them to conduct needs assessments, identify technology resources, provide assistive technology services, and conduct public awareness programs, among others. It also provided definitions of assistive technology devices and services that were added to IDEA in one of its amendments.

When school personnel make decisions about the most appropriate educational program for students with disabilities, IDEA mandates that they must adhere to the following guarantees:

- The child's parents must be notified in writing when the child is to be tested for possible special education placement. They are assigned *due process rights* that ensure procedural safeguards in all matters related to the student's evaluation and educational placement.
- Each student with a disability is entitled to an education in the *least restrictive environment*. This means that, to the extent possible, they should receive education in educational settings designed for students without disabilities.
- Students who are to receive special education services are entitled to an IEP that specifies their strengths and weaknesses, educational goals, objectives, those who are responsible for their education, and dates for reassessment and revision of the IEP. Their parents must be involved in planning for the IEP, as should the student, who will receive educational services to the extent possible.
- The families of students with disabilities should expect *confidentiality and right to privacy* concerning records regarding their children, their school placement, and related activities.
- If the parents of a student with disabilities are unable to be involved in their education planning, they are entitled to the services of a *parent surrogate*.
- Students with disabilities are entitled to free and appropriate special education services until they are 21 years of age.

In addition to the IEPs that are developed for children of school age, preschool children with disabilities are entitled to the development of Individualized Family Service Plans (IFSPs), those who are completing their school careers are entitled to an Individualized Transition Plan (ITP), and those with disabilities who are receiving rehabilitation services are entitled to an Individualized Rehabilitation Plan (IRP). Similar procedures and guarantees are involved in designing and implementing each of those legal rights.

APPENDIX B

A Functional Approach to Individual Differences

A. Edward Blackhurst

Most educators support the goal of responding to the individual differences exhibited by their students. Because of the logistics involved in dealing with large numbers of students, however, most teachers individualize instruction by grouping students with peers who have similar characteristics. Although such practices have produced successful results for most students over the years, teachers often have difficulty responding to students who have unique characteristics that set them apart from "typical" students. A model that can be used to guide decision making and delivery of services for such students is presented in this appendix.

When decisions are being made about the provision of individualized services, a useful perspective is to focus on the problem the student has in functioning within his or her environment. For example, a preschooler with cerebral palsy may lack the fine muscle control that will permit her to fasten buttons so that she can get dressed independently. A boy with a visual impairment may be unable to read printed material that is being used for instruction in an English class. Another student, for unknown reasons, may be unable to solve math problems. Similarly, a child who has been in an automobile accident may have had a severe head injury that has impaired her ability to speak clearly.

In each of these cases, an environmental demand has been placed on the student to perform some function that he or she will find difficult to execute because of a set of unique circumstances or restriction in functional capability caused by the lack of personal resources. For example, the aforementioned children lack the physical or mental capability to button, read, calculate, or speak clearly.

All of us face situations daily in which environmental demands are placed on us. Our goal is to understand the processes and relate them to the lives of students who face more complex and restrictive situations. There is the need to know many things, such as the nature of the demands that are being placed on the student from the environment and how those demands create requirements to perform different human functions, such as learning, walking, talking, seeing, and hearing. It is important to know (1) how such requirements are—or are not—being met by the student and (2) how factors such as the student's perceptions and the availability of personal resources—including intelligence, sight, and mobility—can affect the responses a student can make. It is also important to understand how availability of external supports, such as special education, different types of therapy, and technology can impact on the student's ability to produce functional responses to the environmental demands.

Environmental Adaptation. The environment can be adapted, or the person can adapt to the environment. This category includes functions associated with these adaptations as seen in the performance of many of the activities of daily living, both indoors and outdoors. Examples of functions include driving, food preparation, operation of appliances, and alteration of the living space.

It may be necessary to make a number of modifications to school facilities to accommodate functions in this category. For example, enlarged door knobs, special switches for controlling computers, grabbers to reach items on high shelves, chalkboards and desks that can be raised so that a student in a wheelchair can use them, and ramps to accommodate wheelchairs may be required. Often, assistive technology specialists are called upon to provide help with environmental adaptations.

Learning, Education and Rehabilitation. Functions in this category include those associated with school activities and various types of therapies and rehabilitation processes. Regular class teachers, special education teachers, speech-language therapists, rehabilitation counselors, psychologists, and others may be involved in providing direct services to students. In addition, numerous technologies also may be used within the context of schools. Included may be computer-assisted instruction, audio instructional tapes, print magnifiers, book holders, and other materials and equipment that can facilitate education.

Sports, Leisure, and Recreation. Functions associated with group and individual sports and productive use of leisure time are included in this functional category. The services of a person trained in adapted physical education may provide a valuable resource in this area. In addition, a wide array of equipment and devices can facilitate functions in this category, including balls that emit audible beeps so that children who are blind can hear them, skis specially designed for skiers with one leg, Braille playing cards, and wheelchairs for basketball players who cannot walk or run.

Many more examples of services and devices could be provided, but these illustrate the importance of attending to human functions when planning and implementing education and related services. Also note, with this perspective, that when planning special education services, it is more relevant to focus on the functions that a student can perform and those in which difficulty is experienced than to focus on a diagnostic label or disability category. Such an orientation enables teachers and those providing related services to more directly address a student's needs.

A Unifying Functional Model

The unifying functional model in Exhibit E illustrates the different elements of life associated with a functional approach to education and related services, including the provision of medical, instructional, and assistive technologies. The model is based on the work of Joseph F. Melichar (Blackhurst, 1997). When examining this model, note that the items in each box are meant to be illustrative and not all-inclusive.

Although each student will be unique, the common challenge is to identify and apply the best possible array of education and related services that will provide support, adjustment, or compensation for the student's functional needs or deficits. A variety of responses may be appropriate. For example, Velcro fasteners may be used to replace buttons on garments for the student having difficulty with buttoning. Braille or audio materials may be provided for the student who cannot read conventional print. The student who has difficulty calculating may require specialized, intense, direct math instruction, while the student who cannot talk may need a computerized device that produces speech.

Functional Areas

Students may exhibit individual differences in one or more of several areas of human function. Following are descriptions of some of the most common. Note how technology can be used, and note the roles that specialists can play in providing support services in each of the areas.

Existence. Functions associated with existence are those responses that are needed to sustain life. These functions include feeding, elimination, bathing, dressing, grooming, and sleeping. Special education services, particularly those for preschool children and those with severe disabilities, may focus on teaching students to perform such functions. Special devices such as button hooks, weighted eating utensils, and combs with long handles may be provided to assist students in performing those functions. Assistance in using such devices also may be provided by occupational therapists.

Communication. The reception, internalization, and expression of information are functions included in the category of communication. Communication aids, speech synthesizers, telephone amplifiers, hearing aids, and the services of speech-language pathologists and audiologists might be appropriate to support communication functions.

Body Support, Alignment, and Positioning. Some students need assistance to maintain a stable position or support portions of their body. Braces, support harnesses, slings, and body protectors are useful devices in this functional category, as would be the services of a physical therapist. Other medical personnel also may provide functional supporting services in this category.

Travel and Mobility. Functions in this category include the ability to move horizontally, vertically, or laterally. Wheelchairs, special lifts, canes, walkers, specially adapted tricycles, and crutches can be used to support these functions. Specialists, such as those who provide mobility training for children who are blind, may be called upon to provide services associated with this category.

REFERENCES AND SELECTED BIBLIOGRAPHY

Alliance for Technology Access. (1996). *Computer resources for people with disabilities*. Alameda: Hunter House.
Barry, J., & Wise, B. J. (1996). Fueling inclusion through technology. *School Administrator*, 53(4), 24–27.
Blackhurst, A. E. (1997). Perspectives on technology in special education. *Teaching Exceptional Children*, 29(5), 41–48.
Blackhurst, A. E., & Berdine, W. H. (Eds.). (1993). *An introduction to special education* (3rd ed.). New York: HarperCollins.
Bryant, D. P., & Bryant, R. R. (1998). Using assistive technology adaptations to include students with learning disabilities in cooperative learning activities. *Journal of Learning Disabilities*, 31(1), 41–54.
Council for Exceptional Children. (1998). IDEA 1997: *Let's make it work*. Reston, VA: Author.
Downing, J. E. (1996). *Including students with severe and multiple disabilities in typical classrooms: Practical strategies for teachers*. Baltimore: Brookes.
DuBois, W. P. (1946/1986). *Twenty-One Balloons*. New York: Puffin Books.
Hourcade, J. J., & Parette, J. P. (1997). Family and cultural alert! Considerations in assistive technology assessment. *Teaching Exceptional Children*, 30(4), 40–44.
Lewis, R. B. (1998). Assistive technology and learning disabilities: Today's realities and tomorrow's promises. *Journal of Learning Disabilities*, 31(1), 16–26.
Lindsey, J. (Ed.). (1999). *Technology and exceptional individuals* (3rd ed.). Austin, TX: Pro-Ed.
McGregor, G., & Pachuski, P. (1996). Assistive technology in schools: Are teachers ready, able and supported? *Journal of Special Education Technology*, 13(1), 4–15.
Scherer, M. J., (1993). *Living in the state of stuck: How technology impacts the lives of people with disabilities*. Cambridge, MA: Brookline.

SOME USEFUL WEB SITES

AskERIC: http://ericir.syr.edu/
Adaptive Device Locator System: http://www.acsw.com/
Council for Exceptional Children: http://www.cec.sped.org/home.htm
Conduct on-line ERIC searches: http://ericae.net/scripts/ewiz/amain2.asp
Hyper-ABLEDATA: http://www.trace.wisc.edu/tcel/abeldata/index/html
List of annotated links to numerous special education resources on a variety of topics: http://serc.gws.uky.edu/www/resources/resmenu.html

EXHIBIT A

Caroline's Medical History

Condition	Possible cause	Treatment
Congenital triple amputee: no legs below the knees, no left arm	Mother experienced a stomach virus 30–35 days after conception—circulation between mother and Caroline was disrupted during this time. Development then continued.	Prosthetic legs and left arm, wheelchair with electric lift, physical therapy for walking, surgeries on right hand (due to frequent use of right hand as a crutch)
Moebius syndrome: lifetime facial paralysis, causing difficulties in speaking and an inability to facially express emotion	This syndrome is thought to be genetically linked, possibly passed on to Caroline by a grandmother.	None. While experimental surgery to correct lack of ability to smile has been done on another child suffering from the same syndrome, Caroline has refused surgery for the present time.
Tracheotomy: an incision made in the trachea to allow for breathing when respiration is not possible otherwise	The surgery was performed when Caroline was two months old due to paralyzed vocal cords (most likely due to the Moebius syndrome)	Surgery was performed within the last nine months to close the tracheotomy. However, it was not possible to close it completely, and the surgery wound occasionally reopens when Caroline coughs and clears her throat.
Lack of body cooling system:	Due to the lack of limbs, Caroline's body cannot effectively regulate her body temperature	Caroline must drink continuously through the night to maintain her temperature, and outdoor activities are extremely limited. She must also avoid bright light due to the sensitivity of her eyes.

EXHIBIT B

Speech Pathologist's Report, Fifth Grade

Testing revealed Caroline's language skills are within the range expected for a child of her age. Articulation errors were found to be minimal in single-word productions; conversational speech is more involved with difficulty due to the physical involvement of the oral structure. Improvement in sound production is noted over the three years since this same test was administered to Caroline. Difficulty with /k/ and voiceless /th/ continue to persist, however. Results of the voice worksheet would indicate a severe voice disorder, however, given the nature of the physical involvement present. Caroline's exceptional ability expectations have been evidenced by her ability to overcome the hypernasality, which resulted from the removal of her tonsils.

Caroline is a remarkable young lady, who is well qualified to give us all lessons in spunk and attitude. She does not view herself as being less able than anyone else and is willing and determined to do and try anything. She has never been observed to take advantage of her handicap. Her independence and ability to keep up with everyone else is a tribute to her family who has "done all the right things" and raised her with the same expectations as the rest of the family. It is highly recommended that all individuals who work with Caroline take the time to read her medical history to fully understand all the obstacles that this exceptional individual and her family have endured and overcome.

EXHIBIT C

Caroline's Grade Record

Caroline's grade record shows the deterioration of progress in middle school.

Year in School	Grades
First grade	A—all subjects
Second grade	A/B—all other subjects C—math
Fourth grade	A/B—all other subjects C—math, reading, and social studies
Fifth grade: 1st & 2nd grading periods	A/B—all other subjects C—one subject (unknown)
Fifth grade: 3rd grading period	C—reading, language, and social studies D—math
Fifth grade: 4th grading period	C—reading, social studies, science/health D—math
Sixth grade: 1st grading period	C—math D—reading, social studies, science, and language arts
Sixth grade: 2nd grading period	D—math, reading, language arts F—social studies and science
Seventh grade: 1st grading period	Art: 92 (A) Home economics: 91 (B) Language arts: 88 (B)* Science: 83 (B) Math: 77 (C) Social Studies: 89 (B)

*Note: At the time of the writing of this case, all Caroline's grades had improved to A's and B's.

EXHIBIT D

Caroline's Autobiographical Essay, Sixth Grade

On Saturday, April 30, 1983, I, Caroline Kaye Ellington, was born. I was four pounds and three ounces. I had one hand and no legs.

Before I was born and the doctors got their results, they showed them to my parents and said they thought that my mom needed to get an abortion, and my parents said "no." A few weeks after I was born the doctors told my parents that they thought my parents needed to have a mercy killing. A mercy killing is where you just let the baby die, by not feeding and neglecting it. My parents said "no."

The doctors gave my parents a list of things I couldn't, wouldn't do, and what I'd do to the family. The list included things like: couldn't walk, I'd be mute, deaf, retarded, blind, I'd break up the family, nobody would like me, and I'd be a burden to society. (This is 1996 and none of the above is true.) One day when I was a few months old, Mom put me in a carseat and set me on the counter. There was a guy wallpapering the kitchen when I wiggled myself off the counter. My mom was at the other end of the kitchen cleaning out the pantry. I couldn't cry out loud because I had paralyzed vocal cords, but I was crying. The man was so scared! He went running to Mom screaming. When Mom found me I was laying flat on my face. We all three cried.

My dog, Muffin, who died last April, helped teach me to sit up. I'd hold onto her ear and she'd get up and then I'd let go and sit there for a few seconds. Then I'd fall. She used to always knock me down the steps. Maybe she was telling me to hold on.

When I was two months old I got a tracheotomy. A tracheotomy is something you get when you can't breathe or can't breathe very well. The doctors said I had paralyzed vocal cords.

When I was one year old, I had surgery on my hand, heart, and hips. My heart is on the right side instead of the left side of my chest. They also had to take my teeth out.

Before I was two years old, I learned to walk on prosthetic legs. I was one of the youngest children to do that at the Shriner's Hospital. I even learned to roller skate when I was five.

EXHIBIT E

Blackhurst's Unifying Functional Model

Copyright A. Edward Blackhurst, 1993. Used by permission.

DISCUSSION QUESTIONS

1. Describe Caroline in terms of her physical, social-emotional, and academic development.
   - In what ways are the developmental domains interdependent? Give specific examples from Caroline's case.
   - In what way is Caroline described as similar to typical adolescents?
   - In what way is Caroline described as dissimilar from typical adolescents?
   - Throughout the case, Caroline insists on being independent. How was this helpful to her? How was this problematic?
2. What are the underlying issues in this case?
3. How might the situation appear from the vantage of the following characters?
   - Caroline
   - Mrs. Ellington
   - Mr. Cristoff, special education resource teacher
   - Mr. Willey, Caroline's fifth-grade teacher
   - Ms. Shelton, Caroline's sixth-grade language arts teacher
   - Ms. Johns, the counselor
   - Ms. Ward, sixth-grade social studies teacher
4. Although Caroline's family could have afforded to enroll her in a private school specifically designed to meet the needs of students with disabilities, they chose to place her in an inclusive public school setting. Evaluate this decision.
   - What are the possible benefits of inclusion? For children with special needs? For typically developing children?
   - What are the possible drawbacks? For children with special needs? For typically developing children?
   - Consider whether you think Mr. and Mrs. Ellington made the right decision for their daughter; explain why or why not.
5. Describe Belle Vista's approach to middle school education. Evaluate whether such an approach would be conducive to promoting the inclusion of children with special needs in the regular program. Explain your reasoning in theory and in practice, as evidenced by Caroline's experiences in the sixth and seventh grades.
6. Describe the nature of the communication between various individuals and groups in this case. How effective was this communication? How might it have been made more effective to enhance Caroline's educational experiences? Consider the communication
   - between regular educators and special educators;
   - among the specialists;
   - between the teachers and Caroline's parents;
   - between Caroline and her peers;
   - between elementary school staff and middle school staff;
   - between central office and school.
7. On two occasions in her regular classes, Caroline speaks up about her disability. Compare and contrast the responses by Sheldon and Johns.
   - What are some alternative responses, and with what possible consequences?

8. Consider the quality of instruction in this case. What did the teachers do to adapt their instruction to meet Caroline's needs?
    - How might the teachers have better informed themselves of the nature of Caroline's physical and cognitive disabilities?
    - Does the responsibility to be informed differ between regular and special education teachers?
9. Caroline began to have social problems. What strategies might the teachers have used to help her develop social skills?
    - How effective were the teacher's strategies to promote Caroline's academic progress?
10. Consider the assistive technology that was used. What were the advantages? Disadvantages?
    - What might have been done differently?
11. Ms. Shelton, Caroline's sixth-grade language arts teacher, announced to Caroline's class, "Everyone has a disability, whether it is academic, physical or social. People have to overcome their disabilities and do the best they can with what they have." What do you think she meant by this statement?
    - Do you agree with it?
    - How might *disability* be defined?
    - Is this a useful way to help the other students to understand Caroline's disabilities? Why or why not? What other strategies might have been tried by Caroline's teachers?
    - Ms. Johns asked Caroline to make a presentation to her class to share her feelings about being disabled and how people often treated her differently. For what reasons might this have been a wise move? In what ways might it have backfired?
12. The Individuals with Disabilities Education Act (see Appendix A), a federal law, mandates that parents must be involved in making educational decisions for their children. Consider the role that Caroline's parents played in this case.
    - How effectively did Caroline's parents participate in the decision-making process for their daughter?
    - If you were Caroline's parents, what, if anything, would you have done differently regarding her teachers?
    - When Ms. Johns asked Caroline to make her presentation, Caroline asked her mother to be part of the talk. "I can't do this," replied Mrs. Ellington. "You have to find your own words for this. I can't fight your battles." Why do you think her mother referred to this experience as a battle and not a learning opportunity? Determine whether you agree with Mrs. Ellington's comment, and explain why.
13. Discuss the various factors in Caroline's turn around in grade 7. Which do you consider most important and why?
14. Explore the possible ramifications of removing Caroline from her regular class to join the special education class for one hour a day.
    - How could the assistance she needed have been provided in her regular classroom?

- What are the pros and cons of receiving support from the special education teacher and remaining with the sixth-grade class?
15. What options did her fifth-grade teacher have in providing student assistants to Caroline?
    - How could he have presented an alternate plan to the principal that did not require students to physically move Caroline but still provided assistance for things such as getting books or materials?
    - Should these minor types of assistance have been continued, or did they undermine Caroline's independence?
16. Describe accommodations you could make for Caroline to assist her in school if she were in your class.
17. Consider the analysis of Caroline's need for technology. The decisions seemed to be based on a technology model of assessing need. Use the information in Appendix B to consider another model—a functional model—for understanding individualization.
    - Examine the information about a functional approach to individualization in Appendix B. This section includes specific activities and in-depth application questions for the functional model approach.
    - Using the functional model approach, evaluate the technology devices and services for Caroline. For example, what should happen with the BAT keyboard now?
18. Should Caroline undergo the same operation as Chelsea? What are the pros and cons of this surgery? Who should make this decision?

Questions on Legal Aspects of Special Education

(Examine the special education legal mandates in Appendix A, pp. 70–71.)

1. Why do you think laws such as IDEA and ADA were enacted?
2. How do you think school personnel would have reacted to Caroline prior to the implementation of IDEA?
3. If you were a parent of a student without a disability, how would you react to the fact that Caroline receives an individualized plan for instruction, while your child does not?
4. What types of problems might arise in schools attempting to fulfill the legal mandates to educate students, such as Caroline, in the least restrictive environment? How do you think school personnel might cope with those problems?
5. What benefits have you noticed or heard about in places where the provisions of IDEA have been implemented?
6. What evidence have you seen to indicate that communities are complying with the provisions of ADA? If you have had no direct experience with either IDEA or ADA, what benefits would you anticipate in places where those laws have been implemented? What drawbacks?

CASE 3

Discussion Question	Corresponding INTASC Principle
1	2 The teacher understands how children learn and develop, and can provide learning opportunities that support their intellectual, social, and personal development.
6	6 The teacher uses knowledge of effective verbal, non-verbal, and media communication techniques to foster active inquiry, collaboration, and supportive instruction in the classroom.
	10 The teacher fosters relationships with school colleagues, parents, and agencies in the larger community to support learning and well-being.
8	3 The teacher understands how students differ in their approaches to learning and creates instructional opportunities that are adapted to diverse learners.
9	5 The teacher uses an understanding of individual and group motivation and behavior to create a learning environment that encourages positive social interaction, active engagement in learning, and self-motivation.

CASE FOUR

Arts on the Line

"Are you really concerned about what happens at this school, Ms. Wosoba? Do you care enough about these kids to let them paint in the first grade?" Patsy Cox asked with her arms tightly folded, looking Carolyn Wosoba straight in the eye. It was an intensely muggy August, and Wosoba had barely arrived at Portland Elementary School as its new principal, eager to meet her teachers. She knew of Cox's reputation as an innovator and "master of the teachable moment," but had hardly expected such directness. Wiping the perspiration from her forehead, Wosoba managed a barely audible response: "Sounds fine to me."

Three weeks later Wosoba decided it was time to see Cox in action. At first glance, her classroom looked like a group of Casperlike miniature ghosts, every student was wearing a man's huge white, long-sleeved shirt as a painter's smock—and there was paint everywhere. Cox's smile suggested she seemed genuinely glad for the visit as she gestured for the principal to come closer to the paint pots. "You see why I asked you about painting—the last principal was mad at me all the time." Wosoba's subsequent visits to the classroom showed how effectively Cox used art to promote student success in other areas, such as literacy. She was famous for making beautiful pop-up books where characters in stories practically came alive. She allowed her students to take the books home, and for some it was all they had to read with their parents. Would this dynamic teacher be even more than the new principal had hoped for in creating a schoolwide commitment to long-term arts integration?

THE INTEGRATED CURRICULUM

Portland Elementary School, originally constructed in 1851, is on the outskirts of one of the oldest and least affluent sections of Louisville, Kentucky. The school motto is "Attitude is the mind's paintbrush. It can color any situation." Prominently displayed in the main entrance is a student-produced paper quilt of symmetrical patches of red overlaid with yellow handprints. Such quilt making is emblematic of community involvement in the life of the school. On any given day parent and grandparent volunteers, many skilled in quilt making and other local crafts, sit in quiet hall corners supporting and coaching individual students in their artistic endeavors.

Wosoba eagerly answers the often posed question "How can a school be filled with outstanding student artwork without a full-time art teacher?" "Our steady stream of visitors wants to know how we do it, and my answer is always the same," she said. "Our teachers are interested in and dedicated to making sure students learn in many different ways." With 93% of the student body on free or reduced lunches and a minority population of 20%, Wosoba explains the immense range of Portland's students' learning styles, abilities, and backgrounds. "It's important to me as a principal and to all of the teachers that we expose students to different ways of knowing each subject and multiple ways of learning essential skills and concepts." With Wosoba's arrival and her commitment to art as an essential part of the curriculum, the challenge for the faculty was, "How can we effectively integrate art without a full-time art teacher and with limited funds?"

Building on the faculty's passion for art as a vital form of expression, Wosoba orchestrated the implementation of "Different Ways of Knowing" (DWoK), a constructivist-oriented, arts-infused curriculum that had to be used in conjunction with a multiyear program of professional development. Initially designed for elementary teachers, the curriculum has an interdisciplinary social studies focus. The basic conceptual framework is that key themes provide for integrated learning experiences, and the DWoK materials all support this integration. Activities in language arts, drama, history, math, and art collectively comprise the unit on American Families. For example, in the drama component, each group of students dramatizes a specific daily chore of families moving west in covered wagons, such as unhitching the horses or carrying water.

Although many Kentucky teachers had become understandably skeptical of trendy or new curriculum that failed to meet students' needs, involvement in DWoK was supported by the Portland teachers. The materials and professional development seemed to be quite consistent with insights based on their years of experience as well as with the goals of the state's mandated reforms (see Exhibit A).

One of the distinguishing characteristics of DWoK is its coherent approach to interdisciplinary teaching with a strong emphasis on the arts. Students can make vital connections while developing essential skills in each subject area. Given Kentucky's commitment to authentic assessment, DWoK's performance-based approach to student work was an acceptable fit. Wosoba noted, however, that "missing from the extensive training and materials was a *formal* structure for assessing student learning." On balance, Wosoba did not see this issue as an insurmountable one. The DWoK curriculum did represent a considerable investment, but it had developed a good track record for providing teachers a holistic way of thinking about teaching and the necessary supporting materials, minus some assessments, to make it happen. Given Cox's many years of experience integrating art in her teaching, she was an obvious choice to be one of six teachers who made a three-year commitment to Portland's first DWoK training.

PATSY COX

Red and yellow peonies, like the colors in a Jackson Pollack painting, adorn Cox's classroom. Flower bouquets from her English cutting garden are one more aesthetic detail that contributes to the gallerylike feeling of Portland. What she casually refers to as her lifelong passion for art does more than just infuse her teaching—it is how she lives. Her crocheting and cross stitching could rival some of the best Appalachian crafts, yet Cox is never one to promote her own talents. Showing an earth-toned vest she recently made, she explains, "Yarns intrigue me—their character, feel, and color. I like to see how I can blend the colors and textures."

When Cox began teaching 16 years earlier, she was determined to make art a cornerstone of her teaching despite her lack of formal training—only one undergraduate art history course. "Anyone with dedication can teach art," she insists. Originally a special education teacher, she quickly noticed that her slower learners become more confident when expressing themselves through art. "Younger students are not so frustrated when they can draw a picture of a word they cannot spell or cut out a picture from a magazine to illustrate a word in a sentence," she explained. "Because it worked so well with these students and helped develop their self-esteem, I was confident art could do the same with students of all ability levels."

Cox's multi-age class consists of six-, seven-, and eight-year-olds of all abilities. Her 24 students regularly gather at five kidney-shaped tables, named Monday, Tuesday, and so on, up to Friday. This arrangement supports her extensive use of cooperative learning and art-based activities that are often combined. Moreover, it gives her easy access to each child which is indispensable to her philosophy: "I believe it is my job to help children develop as individuals—to use every opportunity to bring out their unique abilities and skills. At the same time, they need engaging activities to promote their social skills now and for the future. Art projects really do both."

One of Cox's colleagues recalls an example of what she calls Cox's total spontaneity in seizing the teachable moment. "We'd combined our students for an integrated lesson where they were painting pictures based on a book we had just read. So here are 90-plus students all in their huge white painters' smocks painting away. All of a sudden Cox stops everyone and draws the whole room's attention to the work of seven-year-old Monique who had happened to mix blue and yellow. Immediately posting the picture on an easel, Cox asked her to describe exactly what she had done to get such a beautiful green. As a follow-up, Cox spontaneously launched into a discussion of primary and secondary colors while continuously referring to Monique's creation. The other two team members and I—we were just in awe of Cox's earnestness. Monique could have been another Georgia O'Keefe in the making."

Another one of the team members elaborates by saying, "As our team leader, Cox inspires us to be creative, but she is a hard act to follow. She has this gift for reaching those kids who drove the rest of us nuts. As team leader she could have had the cream of the crop, but she always assigned herself to work with the slow readers and kids with problems. It's through art and her creativity that she is successful in reaching all types of students; sometimes I think that by just getting them painting they would listen to her."

Cox views her room as her canvas. Her full-time aide oversees the hands-on art center, located in the corner of the classroom, where children create and mix paints in beachcombing-size pails. The nearby east wall serves as backdrop for the current thematic unit, "Clothing for All Occasions," a topic in which children learn about geography and diversity while developing their art, language, and math skills. Life-size, cut-out clothing of every type and shape makes up the exhibit. Using construction paper for a frame, then stuffing it with crumpled paper from the recycling bin, students then paint the faceless mannequins. Once completed, students intently survey their products, quite pleased with their realistic three-dimensional clothing. After giving them feedback on their creations, Cox placed a price tag on each product in anticipation of a future math lesson for students to compare and contrast "good buys."

Having her own classroom is a recent development for Cox. For several years she and three other teachers team-taught in a pod type classroom with anywhere from 80 to 95 students. When Wosoba assigned all teachers their own rooms, Cox's team elected to continue their collaboration and the regular sharing of ideas, materials, and problems. One team member remarked, "We never know what Cox might be cooking up, but it always keeps us fresh and on our toes." Cox, reflecting on the collaboration, says with a broad grin, "I think we're married." Although the team now does most activities individually, they continued to coordinate lessons for several projects, such as the 16 by 8 foot paper quilt hanging in the main hallway.

"I stay here because of the camaraderie and mutual support we have gained through working together for years," Cox said. "As soon as Wosoba arrived, she fostered team building—she provides opportunities for all team members to attend workshops and meetings together. That's no easy task considering almost all of us commute from suburban communities."

THE SCHOOL

The interior structure of Portland Elementary is the oldest building in Kentucky known to be still in use. The architecture of the downtown neighborhood surrounding the school, located on the Ohio River, suggests that in pre-Depression days this may have been a wealthy area, owing to the ornate post-Victorian facades on several homes and churches. Now, the area has a forlorn quality due to years of decay with little visual relief from the austerity of abandoned warehouses. Despite some deterioration surrounding the school, there is nothing forlorn about this vibrant school community. Renovated in the 1960s, Portland's exterior now consists of large, curving "smokestacks" that flank the glass arched entrance doors, reminiscent of a river steamboat with portholes and paddle wheels (see Exhibit B).

Inside the two-story building, polished hallways bathed in natural light add to the gallery-like ambience. Folk art murals produced by local secondary students capture the history of nineteenth century life in the Portland District. The largest (14 by 6 foot) mural is a scene of a crowded, bustling riverfront, depicting its commercial as well as social importance. Even Portland's passageways conjure up images of the past. Brick rimmed archways connect the school's main areas, all of which converge on the cafe-

An interior mural is framed by one of several rimmed archways that connect Portland's main areas.

teria. The striped awning that hangs over the lunch counters and the pastel colored mural of a convivial street scene give the lunch room the air of a Paris café in a Renoir painting. The lunchroom is also used as the school's "town hall," reinforcing the implicit theme of community.

Working collaboratively, Portland teachers organize historic walking tours to develop students' community pride while they learn history, architecture, and science. Prominent on the tour are designs in the "steamboat" style that were popular along the Ohio and Mississippi Rivers during the Mark Twain era. The walking tours are a permanent resource for teaching essential concepts in a natural environment. In one of Cox's combined math and art lessons, students look for architectural patterns by comparing and contrasting two "shotgun"-style[1] houses that were identical when originally built but are very different today (Exhibit C). "By learning art concepts (like pat-

---

[1] A shotgun house is one in which all the rooms are in a direct line with each other, usually from front to back.

terning) and making connections to math, science, history and language arts as they walk through their neighborhood, students achieve a higher level of focus and remember what they have experienced," Cox explains. Many of the students' families have lived in the area for generations, and the tours give children a new perspective on the value of their architectural legacy.

USING ART FOR MULTIPLE PATHS TO LEARNING

Patsy Cox is a leading proponent of the historic homes tour because, like other Kentucky primary teachers, she focuses on the concept of patterns in her teaching. The historic tour provides an ideal opportunity to extend and apply previous student learning. She begins the year teaching patterns with commercial calendar activities such as the math kit Box It, Bag It.[2] As students select shapes from the bag, such as circles, squares, and triangles representing a different day of the week, they rely on their growing understanding of patterns to predict the next colored shape to emerge.

"I draw on children's natural curiosity to learn shape, color, and sequencing," explained Cox. "These art concepts support the development of the cognitive skills of inferencing and predicting. At first, students work to become comfortable guessing what colored shape will come next in a sequence. As they make more and more correct guesses, I ask them to explain their answers. When they can support their guess with an explanation, I know they are no longer guessing, but are reasoning—truly predicting—based on evidence. Students then apply this ability to identify and differentiate among patterns in a real-world setting during the walking tour. I had students take notes and make drawings of the patterns and shapes found in the architectural styles. Once back in the classroom, the students use the Portland Museum Coloring Book to confirm their findings and learn some architectural terms. For example, they discovered that *fish scales* is a term that describes overlapping thin, flat layers of shingles. They have fun finding other examples from their learning outside the classroom."

With the DWoK curriculum, students test their newfound awareness of similarities and differences in local architecture. Adapting ideas from a social studies module on shelter, children in small cooperative groups designed and built shelters using newspapers, yarn, shingles, garbage bags, masking tape, sticks, and rope. Cox encouraged her student teacher, Donita, to facilitate the activity so that she could become familiar with DWoK material. Impressed with Donita's organization and quality of student-produced shelters, Cox declared the entire process a success. Students were thoroughly absorbed in the task. Initially they focused on taping their desks and chairs together to produce strong foundations for their shelters. As the project progressed, students became more creative and thought of important design features. The objectives of Donita's lesson included collaborating in small groups, producing a product demonstrating some essential aspects of shelter, and showing an understanding of related vocabulary.

---

[2] Available from Math Learning Center, P.O. Box 3226, Salem, OR 97301; (503) 370-8130.

Like Donita, other student teachers assigned to mentors involved in the DWoK process had a positive experience. Subsequently, Donita's professors at the University of Louisville received a grant to integrate DWoK into their early childhood master's program for beginning teacher certification. The philosophical rationale was straightforward: the DWoK materials were thematic, constructivist, and supported the concept that children learn in different ways. In addition, the professors knew their students needed just this type of integrated preparation. The portfolio requirement that student teachers show evidence of using DWoK integration in their lesson planning and/or assessments met with great success.

ASSESSMENT

By February of her first year in DWoK, Cox's response to the curriculum and training program was tepid. "It has given me some useful ideas, but I was already using lots of art-based creative projects. I did not see any curriculum in DWoK that teachers could not develop themselves given enough time and opportunity for collaboration." Cox's curriculum revealed that it was hard to tell where her own activities and materials ended and DWoK began. Was there really anything new about DWoK? However, by the close of the school year, Cox's initial concerns had begun to dissipate—she did acknowledge that DWoK was expanding her thinking about assessment.

Early on, the Kentucky Assessment System (KIRIS), a linchpin of the 1990 reform, had a concerted emphasis on performance assessment. Cox welcomed the new paradigm as a major step toward compatibility with the personalized learning essential to an arts-infused curriculum. Throughout her years of experience, she felt that the almost exclusive use of objective paper-and-pencil tests had deterred regular classroom teachers from cultivating student creativity. DWoK offered some new, albeit informal, avenues for interpreting and appraising students' creative products.

Before her involvement with DWoK, Cox had used oral questions and some anecdotal records to appraise what students learned through creative expression. Extending her own question-and-answer format for viewing student projects, she began using "gallery walks"—an idea she had picked up during DWoK training. In gallery walks, student-made sculptures, posters, and dioramas are arranged to encourage whole-class and visitor viewing. At midyear, Cox's students transformed their environment into a tropical paradise for a parent-attended gallery walk. Student research on Hawaii yielded gallery decorations such as clay sculptures of molten lava volcanoes and cascading waterfalls. Also on display were hula skirts made of newspaper and Hawaiian fruit made of papier-mâché.

Hand-in-hand, parents and students strolled through the tropical paradise, pausing in front of each student's creation, listening to the artist's brief report on the history, culture, and economy of the 49th state. Cox used these oral reports and student answers to audience questions for her final assessment.

Cox explained, "This method proves useful in assessing reading comprehension and retention and is also applicable to any unit of study. When a student explains his or her creation, the depth of knowledge and understanding which prompts accurate and appropriate connections comes shining through." In the case of the Hawaiian gallery walk, each guest participated in a grand finale: a luau with sumptuous Hawaiian food.

Portland parents, who frequently assist in their children's research gathering, eagerly participate in the gallery walks. Patsy discovered some surprising benefit from parent involvement in the art projects. "They serve as catalysts for students to spend quality time with their parents. I remember one little boy in my first year of DWoK, David, rarely received much attention at home because his mother was tired and felt overworked," Cox said. "His excitement and enthusiasm for school projects energized his mother, giving her the impetus to spend 'special' time with him."

Another DWoK-inspired gallery walk focuses on the hardships and sacrifices of pioneers in the 1800's. The pioneer theme is captured in *The Josefina Story Quilt* (Coerr, 1986), one of the many books accompanying the DWoK curriculum. In choosing this story, Cox builds on students' prior knowledge of families as well as their understanding of quilt making. As she makes her way through the gallery walk viewing creations the story inspired, she asks students questions such as "What does this part of your quilt convey about pioneer life?" Their answers help Cox evaluate the depth of their understanding of the key themes.

A NEW WAY OF THINKING ABOUT AND EXPANDING ASSESSMENT

Despite Cox's original lukewarm response to the DWoK curriculum, she ardently points out that her second year of participation in DWoK caused a change in her thinking. Initially she had conceived art integration too narrowly, confining it only to social studies and science. By year 2 she was eager to experiment using art to enhance mathematical understanding as well. Inspired by activities about ethnic foods in the DWoK module on America's Family Stories, Cox's class conducted an ice cream survey, a hands-on project involving everyone at Portland. Her students canvassed the school, asking teachers, staff, and students if they preferred chocolate, strawberry, or vanilla ice cream. Students learned to graph the results and display them on a large sheet of construction paper tacked on the hallway wall adjacent to their class. Sections on the graph paper matched the color of flavors surveyed. Students created true-to-life paper ice cream cones representing the number of people choosing each flavor, drawing upon students' understanding of color, form, and line to present survey data publicly. Since the graphs were essentially pictographs, they were assessed based on accuracy. Did students use the correct colors, accurate numbers, and shapes of the ice cream cones according to the graph key?

As the second year of her DWoK program continued, Cox further expanded her approaches to appraising student work. Convinced of the importance of self-assessment, she wanted students to see for themselves the processes involved in their own thinking. Her newest approach was to have students work independently or with a buddy, chronicling in their journals the specific steps taken in developing a project. Students eagerly scrutinized the journals during both self- and peer review.

Cox creates a loom from oversize construction paper for a hands-on weaving lesson to help students develop their understanding of spatial relationships.

"Kids are honest and are quite able to define similarities and differences between compositions, a key cognitive skill," Cox noted. "Journal writing and peer review, when matched with teacher assessment, provided checks and balances for emerging student insights." She also kept index cards for recording student progress concerning self-reflection in the following areas: collaboration with peers, approach to the artistic process, and the final product. She embraced this multidimensional strategy as a holistic method for detecting students' strengths and areas for improvement.

The DWoK program refers to the process of keeping anecdotal records as "kid-watching"—a procedure Cox uses while teaching the "clothing in literature" theme. After she reads her students the richly illustrated book A *New Coat for Anna* (Ziefert, 1986), she leads them in a weaving project drawing on essential themes and weaving processes learned from the story. As Cox demonstrates how to fold and cut the paper, she has the students' rapt attention. "Why are the shops empty? How do Anna and her mother dye her coat red? What is the name for the yarns that go up and down on the loom?" Many hands go up, and Cox smiles broadly hearing the correct answer "weft". When Cox does not receive a particular answer she is looking for, she encourages them: "Think about the question while you work and perhaps the answer will become clear." One student, Benjamin, pondered his weaving project. With only two strips of colored paper woven through, he knew something was wrong. He pulled the last blue strip out and tried to weave it back in the same way, but again, he saw that it was still wrong. Undaunted, Ben tried one more time, and success was obvious by the big grin on his face.

Through "kid watching," Cox followed Ben through each attempt to rework his paper weaving, and was pleased with the DWoK system as a major improvement over her index cards. She noted as part of her anecdotal records his perseverance, risk-tak-

Table 4.1
Overview of Kid-Watching Forms (see Exhibit D for complete forms)

Name of Form	Objectives	Areas of Focus
The process of learning	Coming to know	• Engagement • Collaboration • Flexibility
The products of learning	Showing you know	• Understanding content • Conventions and forms • Presentations
Reflections	Knowing you know	• Where we've been • Where we go next

ing, problem-solving, and revision strategies. At various times Cox used all three "kid-watching" forms developed by DWoK to collect and organize assessment information about her students.

By the end of her second year with DWoK, Cox was exhilarated with her expanded repertoire for student assessment. "Continuing kid watching while adding strategies for self-assessment is ideal for a multi-age classroom—it helps me efficiently organize and plan lessons to meet the needs of all my students," stated Cox. "When I ask students how well they are meeting a particular goal, their responses show me not only what they think of their work, but also what they were doing, and why. They really had quite a bit to say. I've come a long way in my thinking about assessment. I know DWoK is in the process of developing specific assessment rubrics and I am hopeful I can go even further in the future."

A PRINCIPAL LOOKS BACK

During what would have been Cox's third and final year in DWoK training, she surprised everyone when she announced she had accepted a position as an intern principal at another local elementary school, a goal she had been working toward for several years. Despite Wosoba's strong support for Cox's professional advancement, she could not hide her disappointment. Cox was not only an outstanding teacher, but as a DWoK team leader she was vital to the mission of arts infusion. If Cox accepted a full-time principalship the following year, what would happen with the DWoK team and the years of colleagueship? There were other issues facing the school as well. If Cox did not return, a new full-time teacher would be needed. If there were no applicants experienced with DWoK, would Portland have the financial resources to send the new teacher for training? Would she ever catch up? Could anyone? If not, how would a newcomer approach art integration and how would this affect Cox's former team?

EPILOGUE

Patsy Cox gazes out of the picture window of her remodeled and spacious wood-paneled office at Hartstern Elementary. "While still new to the role of principal, I am confident in my ability to support teacher innovation." Approving the agenda for an upcoming in-service day, Cox smiled as she displayed the list of several teachers who were signed up for training in the "Different Ways of Knowing" program. Her own successful experience propelled her enthusiasm for encouraging Hartstern teachers in the use of DWoK curriculum. She believed the timing was vital since Kentucky had recently formalized a fine arts assessment for fifth, eighth, and eleventh grades. One nagging concern dampened her enthusiasm—the success of DWoK would require more than just a handful of enthusiastic teachers and her active involvement as principal. How would she foster the colleagueship she knew to be at the heart of systemic reform? Given her own success with Donita, she had counted on having some DWoK-trained student teachers from the University of Louisville to be part of her team-building approach. However, the university-based DWoK program had lapsed when the grant ran out.

Wistfully, Cox thought about her 10 years as a primary teacher at Portland Elementary. The urban school, bordered by unending blocks of abandoned warehouses, offered such a sharp contrast to the gentle landscape surrounding Hartstern, reminiscent of an Andrew Wyeth painting. What had kept her at Portland and made art integration such an exciting journey was the friendships—the intense sense of collegiality where "one for all and all for one" was axiomatic. How effective would she be in trying to re-create that experience for teachers at Hartstern, teachers who worked so successfully as individuals?

Cox's three former team members have continued to share and collaborate on occasional projects, but things are not the same at Portland. According to one teacher, "It's been some time now, and we have never had the fun and teamwork we had with Patsy Cox."

REFERENCES AND SELECTED BIBLIOGRAPHY

Belk, J. A., & Calais, G. J. (1993). *Portfolio assessment in reading and writing: Linking assessment and instruction to learning.* Paper presented at the annual meeting of the Mid South Educational Research Association, New Orleans, LA (ED 365 732).

Coerr, E. (1986). *The Josefina story quilt.* New York: Harper Trophy Harper Collins.

Coeyman, M. (1999, February 2). Spelling—and art: History—and art. *Christian Science Monitor,* 4–5.

Gardner, H. (1993). *Multiple intelligences: The theory in practice.* New York: Basic Books.

Giles, C., Andre, M., Dye, C., & Pfannenstril, V. (1998). Teaching about books: Constant connections through literature—using art, music, and drama. *Language Arts,* 76(1), 27–34.

Goodlad, J., & Anderson, R. (1987). *The nongraded elementary school* (rev. ed.). New York: Teachers College Press.

Katz, L. (1993). What can we learn from Reggio Emilia? In C. P. Edwards, G. Forman, & L. Gandiani (Eds.), *The hundred languages of children: The Reggio Emilia approach to early childhood education* (pp. 19–37). Norwood, NJ: Ablex.

Kellogg, R. (1970). *Analyzing children's art*. Palo Alto, CA: Mayfield.

Kellogg, R. (1979). *Children's drawings, children's minds*. New York: Avon.

Korzenik, D. (1973-74). Role-taking and children's drawings. *Studies in Art Education*, 15(3), 17–24.

Leeds, J. A. (1986). Teaching and the reasons for making. *Art Education*, 39(7), 17–21.

Newsom, B. Y., & Silver, A. Z. (1978). *The art museum as educator*. Berkeley: University of California Press.

Thompson, C. A. (1995). Transforming curriculum in the visual arts. In S. Bredekamp & T. Rosegrant (Eds.), *Reaching potentials: Transforming early childhood curriculum and assessment* (Vol. 2, pp. 81–98). Washington, DC: National Association for the Education of Young Children.

Wertsch, J. (1990). The voice of rationality in a sociocultural approach to mind. In L. Moll (Ed.), *Vygotsky and education: Instructional implications and applications of sociohistorical psychology* (p. 114–126). New York: Cambridge University Press.

Ziefert, H. (1986). *A new coat for Anna*. New York: Alfred Knopf.

EXHIBIT A

Overview of Different Ways of Knowing (DWoK)

The "Different Ways of Knowing" curriculum was developed by the Galef Institute.[1] As of 1999, it has been implemented in schools in 13 states: Alabama, Arizona, California, Florida, Hawaii, Kentucky, Michigan, Mississippi, Montana, New Jersey, Oregon, Texas, and Washington. The most extensive effort, however, has been in Kentucky where it has expanded to include at least 40% of all elementary schools in two-thirds of the state's districts.

The Collaborative for Teaching and Learning, located in Louisville, Kentucky, supports classroom reform with the DWoK curriculum and accompanying professional development. The collaborative offers the three-year DWoK course of study to school teams of teachers and administrators. Professional development includes:

- Music, visual arts, drama, dance, science, and mathematics
- Yearlong technical assistance and on-site coaching in the classroom
- Curriculum materials for teachers and students
- Newsletters, access to an interactive Web site (DWoKNET)

An evaluation of DWoK (Hovda, R., & Kyle, D. [1997], *Different Ways of Knowing: Effects on teaching and learning practices*, Louisville, KY: University of Louisville) in 24 Kentucky elementary schools concluded that when the entire faculty participated in DWoK for at least two years:

- DWoK changed teachers' knowledge, attitudes, and beliefs about how young children learn.
- DWoK changed teachers' instructional practices to accommodate differences in students learning styles and strengths.
- Students in DWoK schools showed improvements in academic performance.
- Students in DWoK classrooms had better attitudes toward school and learning than students who did not participate in DWoK.
- DWoK helped increase collaboration among teachers, making school a more vibrant learning community.

---

[1] Contact Sue Beauregard or Amy Berfield, The Galef Institute, 11050 Santa Monica Blvd., Third Floor, Los Angeles, CA 90025-3594; phone, (310) 479-8883; E-mail, sue@galef.org or amy@galef.org.

For more about Different Ways of Knowing in Kentucky, contact:

Dr. Linda Hargan, Executive Director
Collaborative for Teaching and Learning
3101 Breckinridge Lane, Suite 1B
Louisville, KY 40220
Phone: (502) 451-3131
E-mail: linda@ky-dwok.org

EXHIBIT B

Portland Elementary School

EXHIBIT C

Shotgun Make-Over

From the Portland Museum Coloring Book. Copyright Portland Museum, Inc. 1989. All rights reserved. Funded by Jefferson County Public Schools.

Shotgun Make-Over
3518 and 3522 Northwestern Parkway

Many years ago, these two houses looked just alike. They were probably built by the same person. Today they are very different. How many things can you find that are similar? How many things are different?

EXHIBIT D

DWoK Kidwatching Forms

STUDENT'S NAME: Jessica

Coming To Know
The Process of Learning

DATE	LEARNING EVENT	ENGAGEMENT • pleasure and involvement • perseverance • risk-taking • responsibility	COLLABORATION • thoughts expressed • openness to feedback • use of input • group work	FLEXIBILITY • modalities used • problem-solving strategies • revision strategies
10/13	Wheel 2: Cluster 3 Exploring Forests (audiotape)	• Excited about new (unknown) project • Listened intently to audiotape • Made predictions	• Shared her predictions • Listened to other's predictions	• Changed some predictions after listening to others • Added details to sketches
3/18	Wheel 2: Cluster 5 Exploring Deserts (pointillism art)	• Read background information pointillism • Listened to others as they read • Looked at models	• Listened to other's comments/observations • Shared her observations • Worked with group to make collage	• Changed her piece of collage (revision) • Experimented with mixing points to create colors.

Kidwatching Form 1

Different Ways of Knowing. Copyright © 1994 The Galef Institute.

Case 4

STUDENT'S NAME Jessica

Showing You Know
The Products of Learning

DATE	LEARNING EVENT	UNDERSTANDING CONTENT • verbal and nonverbal expressions of main idea	CONVENTIONS AND FORMS • first uses of conventions • practiced use of conventions	PRESENTATION • clarity • detail • focus • purpose • voice
10/13	Wheel 2: Cluster 3 Exploring Forests (forest bags)	• Is able to explain why she made the predictions/observations that she made • Drew pictures of content of bags	• Used both pictures and words to express thoughts • Lists items in the bags	• Explained predictions in a clear voice • Included details - focused on purpose
3/18	Wheel 2: Cluster 5 Exploring Deserts (pointillism)	• Quickly began placing points on paper • Was able to explain her thinking about the collage piece.	• Worked to make her part of the collage "perfect" • Tried to make her piece "fit" into collage	• Able to explain why she constructed her collage in the way she did • Collage piece is focused + detailed

Kidwatching Form 2

Different Ways of Knowing. Copyright © 1994 The Galef Institute.

Arts on the Line   103

STUDENT'S NAME Jessica

Knowing You Know
Reflections

The essence of education may well be the ability to look back on the learning experience and evaluate what worked and why, and what didn't work and why. Self-reflection—thinking about learning—helps students discover what they have learned, how they learned it, and what they should do next to extend and refine their learning. Please duplicate the *Learning About My Learning* student self-reflection form (on the other side of this form) and use it whenever you feel it is appropriate. Your students' self-reflections will help you plan instruction and create curriculum that will best support them.

DATE	LEARNING EVENT	WHERE WE'VE BEEN • the learner's plan for learning • the learner's strengths	WHERE WE GO NEXT • the learner's needs
10/14	Wheel 2: Cluster 3 Exploring Forests	• Wants to study mangrove trees because she's never heard of them before. • Plans to use electronic encyclopedia and tree books for research	• Help her focus research on location and appearance.
3/19	Wheel 2: Cluster 5 Exploring Deserts	• Wants to know more about saguaro cactus • Interested in Seurat after learning about pointillism	• Help her find books on the saguaro cactus

Kidwatching Form 3

Different Ways of Knowing. Copyright © 1994 The Galef Institute.

DISCUSSION QUESTIONS

1. Describe the environment at Portland Elementary.
   - What is the school's general attitude toward education?
   - What is its relationship with the community?
   - What are some unique features of the teaching/learning environment?
2. Describe Patsy Cox as a teacher.
   - What is her teaching philosophy? Has it changed over time?
   - How has Cox's interest in the arts evolved?
   - Discuss her use of questioning and its value or lack of for producing higher-order thinking.
3. Faced with the lack of a comprehensive art integration program, Portland chose to purchase the DWoK program. Cox initially reports that with adequate time, the teachers could have developed similar activities on their own.
   - What are some other alternatives the school could have pursued to achieve art integration? With what consequences?
   - When a school lacks the resources to implement a program such as DWoK, can teachers successfully integrate art? If so, how?
4. When a school such as Portland invests money and training into a specific curriculum program, what issues need to be taken into consideration?
   - What issues arise when a new teacher with no DWoK training joins a faculty team that is using DWoK?
   - What is an individual teacher's responsibility to the team?
   - What are some possible outcomes for Portland's pending art program given Cox's decision to become an administrator?
   - What would you do in Cox's situation?
5. How does successful arts integration occur?
   - What is the role of the individual teacher? The school administrators?
   - Discuss the classroom teachers' responsibility to the arts with and without a full-time art teacher.
6. What are various ways of assessing student art? Discuss the pros and cons of each.
   - To what degree should assessment be based on anecdotal records and student self-assessment alone?
   - To what extent does Cox use art or graphics to assess learning in various content areas?
7. How did Cox's approach to assessment change over the time period captured in the case?
   - How realistic was her ultimate approach to assessment?
   - What would you do the same and what would you do differently? Why?
8. From Cox's viewpoint, a strong sense of collegiality is vital to the success of arts integration.
   - Do you agree or disagree? If you agree discuss in detail specific kinds of colleagueship that should occur.
   - How can teachers/administrators make this happen?

9. Although Portland did not have its own art teacher, it had three vital resources that did not involve additional funding: (1) a historic community, (2) high parent involvement, and (3) strong teacher teams.
    - Discuss the relative importance of each of these for art integration.
    - What other resources could facilitate the process?
10. Cox says, "Anyone with dedication can teach art."
    - Do you agree or disagree with this statement?
    - How might a trained art teacher respond?
    - What are the strengths and drawbacks of Cox's position?
11. What benefits are achieved through the use of art in Cox's classroom? Are there drawbacks?
    - For the teacher
    - For the student
    - For the parent

CASE 4

Discussion Question	Corresponding INTASC Principle
2	**4** The teacher understands and uses a variety of instructional strategies to encourage students' development of critical thinking, problem solving, and performance skills.
6	**8** The teacher understands and uses formal and informal assessment strategies to evaluate and ensure the continuous intellectual, social, and physical development of the learner.
7	**9** The teacher is a reflective practitioner who continually evaluates the effects of his/her choices and actions on others (students, parents, and other professionals in the learning community) and who actively seeks out opportunities to grow professionally.
8, 9	**10** The teacher fosters relationships with school colleagues, parents, and agencies in the larger community to support learning and well-being.
11	**3** The teacher understands how students differ in their approaches to learning and creates instructional opportunities that are adapted to diverse learners.

CASE FIVE

"I Don't Think I Can Teach This Again"

"I just don't know if I'm prepared to teach *Huck Finn* again. This book has caused so much dissension and heartache," Leslie Jenkins confided to her good friend and colleague, Helen Benroe. Despite the fact that both were veteran teachers and had taught the book before, Benroe nodded sympathetically.

Jenkins and Benroe were attending a weeklong summer conference at The Mark Twain House, a museum in Hartford, Connecticut, dedicated to the study and celebration of the life and works of Samuel Clemens. More than thirty teachers from around the country had gathered to talk and think about how to teach *Adventures of Huckleberry Finn* in the 1990s.

The scholars at The Mark Twain House did not want this classic text, the most frequently taught novel in American schools (Carey-Webb, 1993), to become a victim of cultural conflicts. Instead, they believed *Huck Finn* was a valuable tool in the war to fight racism. Jenkins' goal was to sort out some of the issues in the novel that had caused such controversy in a nearby district. She hardly wanted a repeat of that situation, but neither did she want to give up teaching this classic.

One of the most banned books in America since its publication in 1884, *Huck Finn* was not new to controversy. It was first banned as coarse and immoral "trash" in 1885 in Concord, Massachusetts (Champion, 1991). In the more recent past, there had been efforts to remove the book from school curricula in such disparate places as Virginia, Texas, and Washington, DC.

Closer to home, the issue of whether to teach *Huck Finn* had exploded a few months earlier at a middle school in Sandbury, a racially diverse Connecticut city about an hour's drive from The Mark Twain House. The parent of an African-American student raised objections when an eighth-grade English teacher was teaching the novel in that school for the eighth time. Although the teacher and school principal tried to explain their educational rationale for teaching *Huck Finn*, concern grew. African-American parents objected in particular to the use of the word "nigger" more than 200 times in the novel. After all, many questioned, how would Jews react if their children had to read a book in which the word "kike" appeared over and over? Would Italian American parents tolerate it if their children were required to read a book that used the term "wop" more than 200 times? Parents of diverse backgrounds were sympathetic to this point of view. Several believed that Twain's novel negatively stereotyped African Americans as superstitious, uneducated, passive, and childlike, and they believed this portrayal threatened to undermine the self-esteem of black youths. One African-American parent complained that her son had been upset when he overheard white classmates mimicking the dialect of Jim, a slave (see Exhibit A).

Parents expressed other opinions as well. Instead of condemning the novel, many praised it for exposing the evils of racism. They perceived Jim as the most noble and sympathetic character in the story. Others maintained that, while the book might be an important literary work, eighth graders were not intellectually mature enough to understand Twain's sophisticated satire. Some parents complained of being bulldozed; they believed it had been impossible for parents to discuss openly the pros and cons of teaching the novel for fear of being labeled racist. And yet another group of parents was flatly opposed to censorship (see Exhibit B for opposing positions).

Two middle-school parents aired their criticisms on a local radio station; soon, the wire services had picked up the story, which appeared in national newspapers and on national television. Interest in the novel seemed to peak around this time, when *The New Yorker* (1996) published a newly discovered episode of *Huck Finn* as well as commentaries by several novelists and critics about Twain and his novel.

Halfway through teaching *Huck Finn*, the English teacher at the Sandbury middle school was ordered to stop until the school system could determine how to respond to parents' concerns. Finally, the superintendent made a decision to remove *Huck Finn* from the eighth-grade curriculum, contending that it was tearing the school apart along racial lines. Since students would still be able to borrow the book from their school library, the superintendent averred that this was a curriculum issue and not a case of censorship.

A few months later, Jenkins and Benroe were attending the conference at The Mark Twain House, listening to David Bradley, an African-American professor of English from Temple University, discuss the controversy that had swirled around *Huck Finn* since its publication. He argued that the work served to remind Americans of the racism in our society, then and now. He quoted Ernest Hemingway, who claimed that all American literature came from *Huck Finn*. Discussing the use of the word "nigger," Bradley asked, "Isn't the classroom the safest place for a child to encounter a potentially harmful word—and in the hands of a skilled teacher, instead of on the playground?" (Schuster, 1995, p. A3)

Bradley, nonetheless, readily admitted the difficulties in teaching *Huck Finn*. Teachers knowledgeable about Twain, *Huck Finn*, and its historical period had to teach students how to read carefully. The context was unfamiliar, the dialects difficult, the satire complex, and the various points of view confusing. This was not a book for beginning readers and could aggravate problems in a class or school already experiencing racial tensions.

Jenkins was both intrigued and worried as she listened to the speaker. Would she be up to teaching this controversial novel to her class of "average" eighth graders in her suburban town? Although she understood the concerns of those who considered the book racist, her stance was that it was not.

LESLIE JENKINS

"From the time I was young, I knew I wanted to be a teacher," Jenkins said. At college, her student teaching experience was a disaster, however. Her master teacher, a seventy-year-old veteran, had decided not to retire and had difficulty relinquishing control. "When she thought I was doing something wrong," Jenkins said, "she'd jump up and say, 'No, no, sit down and watch me do it.' I lost credibility with the students and felt incompetent. My college supervisor was supportive and promised to pass me as long as I tried, but that's not the way I ever wanted to do anything—just getting by."

After that experience, Jenkins took a break from the classroom. A year later, she was hired to teach English and reading to middle schoolers in a small private school. There, colleagues took her under their wing, and she thrived. At the same time, she completed her master's degree in teaching, gaining new strategies to practice in her classroom.

After three years, Jenkins and her husband Robert decided to start a family. She taught part-time when her two children were young. Jenkins had now been teaching full-time at Webster Middle School for four years.

THE SCHOOL AND COMMUNITY

Webster Middle School was nestled into the gently rolling countryside of Hillsdale, a town of approximately fifteen thousand. Once a cluster of farms, this upper-middle-class community was dotted with homes valued as high as a million dollars. In most of the two-parent families, both parents worked as professionals—doctors, lawyers, and insurance executives. In a corner of the town, there was a small development of subsidized apartments for low-income families.

Many Hillsdale residents worked in Oldtown, a city of 130,000 located thirty minutes away. A stark contrast to Hillsdale, Oldtown reflected the fate of many major northeastern cities as it struggled with decaying factories, aging schools, a high level of poverty, and a fleeing middle class. Still, its many cultural institutions, excellent restaurants, and lively nightlife continued to draw citizens from around the state.

While approximately 90 percent of the public school population in Oldtown was minority, suburban Hillsdale was almost completely white. There were only a few African-American children at Webster Middle School and some children from Asian backgrounds. There was one synagogue in town; most families belonged to mainstream Christian denominations.

Webster Middle School was a modern structure accented by circular windows and interior communal spaces with conferencing tables for students and teachers to meet in small groups. It had about 180 students per grade level, with classes typically of 18 to 20 students. Webster was proud of its fine academic reputation.

THE CLASS

Jenkins taught three sections of eighth-grade English. The school was on a six-day schedule. Half the periods were forty-five minutes, and half were ninety-minute sections. Jenkins valued the longer sessions because they gave time to focus in greater depth on a topic; however, it was sometimes hard for eighth graders to sustain their attention.

Although her preparations were seemingly identical, the three sections were tracked and moved at different paces. Jenkins preferred working with the middle-level students. "I like the 'average' kids because it's a challenge to try to reach them," she said. "The diversity of ability levels and learning styles keeps me on my toes, thinking of new and creative ways to reach them." Her favorite group this year, the lively fourth period class, had twenty-one students. Two-thirds of the class worked just at the mastery level and one-third at slightly below mastery level in reading and writing. There were six students who had been identified as having attention deficit disorder (ADD), two who were learning disabled (LD), and one who was identified as having behavior disorders. Many of the children had stepparents, and three were from single-parent families. All of the children were white, except Sandra, an African American.

Jenkins called this highly animated, social group her "runaway train." She felt a great responsibility to spur their enthusiasm and not to harness them by working too hard to "keep them in line." But the class met right before lunch, when the six students with ADD had just about run through their medication. Jenkins found that she constantly had to change their seats to try to keep them focused. When she succeeded in keeping them involved, they followed through and often challenged her intellectually. "I think several of these students are very bright and stimulate the others. Even the less capable students come up with wonderful thoughts," she remarked.

JENKINS' REASONS FOR TEACHING *HUCK FINN*

Jenkins explained why she had chosen to teach *Huck Finn*. "A few years ago, the eighth-grade teachers and the language arts coordinator decided that it was a key text that should be taught. Now our students read it after studying *To Kill a Mockingbird* to continue the themes of growth, maturity, and discrimination. During the year, they also read Steinbeck's *Of Mice and Men* and several short stories. Although *Huck Finn* is a requirement, I could avoid it if I wished. Some teachers say they don't have enough time, since it's taught at the end of the year. But I feel that *Huck Finn* is an important book. I always try to make connections so students see a book's relevance to their own lives. I've admitted to the kids that I feel some apprehension because of its controversial aspects. It's a stretch for me, but we're going to be learning together. If the students are really turned on, they'll gain new insights that I never thought of and that I can bring to future students."

After taking the summer seminar at The Mark Twain House, Jenkins was enthusiastic about teaching *Huck Finn* again. Although Jenkins had taught it twice before, she felt she needed a better connection to the novel to teach it well. She was familiar with the names of the scholars who were speaking at the conference and eager to hear them.

She was also motivated by concern. She had read newspaper accounts about the Sandbury middle school controversy and wanted to find out more about the issues and possible objections to the novel. After she attended the conference, if parents expressed concerns about *Huck Finn* at Webster, she would be better able to address these.

In the past, Webster parents had seemed pleased by the idea that their middle schoolers were reading a text frequently taught at the high school and college levels. Jenkins speculated that they saw this as a sign of their children's ability. But now that the Sandbury incident was known all over the state, she wondered how the parents would respond.

PREPARING STUDENTS TO READ THE NOVEL—MID-APRIL

After attending the conference, Jenkins approached the novel differently. Previously, she had focused primarily on plot (see Exhibit C for plot summary). Although she had spent some time discussing the themes of the text, she now decided to explore these much more fully and to help her students understand Twain's literary techniques, including his satire and irony.

Holding up a new copy of *Huck Finn*, Jenkins introduced the novel by discussing how controversial it had always been. Sharing quotes from the scholars at the conference, she asked students to read them over and try to paraphrase the scholars' concerns in their own words. She wanted students to consider seriously whether they might not want to read it. She explained that she was still learning about the novel and was offended by certain aspects of it, such as the use of the word "nigger". Then she posed a challenge: "Some people don't think middle schoolers are ready to read this book. There's offensive language in it, the dialect is hard, and the satire is difficult. It's obvious that the district thinks you're up to it, but what do you think?" she asked her students.

The combination of their teacher's challenge and the new books sparked the students' interest. The student with a behavior disorder, an avid reader, suggested passing out the book before the upcoming spring vacation for those students who wanted to get a head start. Twelve out of the twenty-one students hurried to the desk to pick up their copies. Although Jenkins originally had intended to provide more historical background information before the students began reading, she decided to let them follow their own interests.

To introduce the theme of racism in *Huck Finn* after spring break, Jenkins had the students read a short story by Angelica Gibbs titled "The Test." In the story, a young black woman is treated in a demeaning fashion by the white man giving her a driver's test. When she loses her composure and confronts him, he fails her on the test. Through group discussion, Jenkins's students readily understood his abuse of power and the racist intent of his comments.

She thought that students would understand the novel better if they were knowledgeable about Clemens' background. For fun, she asked them to collect and share ten interesting facts about the author. Students dug up information about Clemens's work as a newspaper reporter and a riverboat pilot.

To prepare students to understand the author's voice in *Huck Finn*, she shared primary materials she had received at the conference supporting the position that Clemens was not a racist. These included a letter from Clemens to the Yale Law School offering to pay the tuition of Warner T. McGuinn, a black student. Students also read a story Clemens wrote that satirically condemned the stoning of Chinese men in San Francisco. They discussed how Clemens capitalized on the power of satire to express his outrage at the mistreatment of others. To introduce the character of Huck, Jenkins gave students Chapter 6 of *The Adventures of Tom Sawyer* in which Twain first presents Huck in his writings. They read about Huck as the juvenile pariah of the town.

Jenkins related *Huck Finn* to an interdisciplinary unit on the study of a local river. She and the science teacher supervised the students' building of seaworthy, biodegradable model rafts and then took them to the river to test the rafts.

STARTING THE NOVEL

Once students began reading the book, they used their journals to document their observations (Exhibit D). Jenkins asked them to start making observations about the characters. They discussed the distinction between Huck's voice as the narrator and Twain's point of view. Through this process, students began to understand that Huck does not always understand what he is reporting.

Jenkins worked to help students understand the characters' dialects. "It's almost like learning a foreign language. By reading passages aloud, students got a sense of the cadence. When they began to understand the meaning of the language, they loved it and felt a real sense of accomplishment," she said.

To facilitate students' understanding of the context of the story, they discussed the characters' superstitions. They recognized that many of these were grounded in common sense and revealed the characters' closeness to nature. The class compared ancient and modern superstitions and created posters representing them.

One of Jenkins's main goals was to make connections between her students' lives and Huck's life, so that the story would have personal meaning for them. The students compared Pap Finn's expectations of Huck to their parents' expectations of them. They questioned a town's responsibility to intervene if a parent is neglectful, comparing Huck's situation to examples of present-day child abuse and neglect.

TEACHING PERSUASIVE WRITING

For the eighth-grade state mastery test, students had to be able to write a persuasive essay, Jenkins decided to integrate the teaching of this skill with the teaching of *Huck*

Finn. She asked students to write a persuasive essay to convince a jury who should be Huck's guardian—Pap, the Widow Douglas, the Judge, or Huck himself.

After writing their essays, the students presented them as speeches in class. Students took notes during each speech and then provided verbal feedback to the speaker, analyzing the persuasive strategies used (Exhibit E). In a variety of ways, each speaker exhorted the jury to protect Huck from his father's abuse.

Then, Jenkins concluded the lesson. "I'm very proud of you. You used the persuasive techniques that a great debater would use—rhetorical questions, cause and effect, good comparisons, and evidence and examples from the book. And you certainly got people's attention with lively images, like 'Pap Finn sleeps with the pigs and the only time he comes to church is to steal the wine.'"

Driving home that afternoon, Jenkins mused that the topic of child neglect and abuse seemed to engage and challenge her students, whereas racism, the issue that had fired the Sandbury controversy, hardly raised a stir. "I'm not sure that's good," she thought.

Moreover, there had been no concerned calls from parents. Jenkins speculated that, since parents in this primarily white community considered themselves open-minded, as a group they would not be likely to feel offended by the novel. Were the responses of students and parents in Hillsdale and Sandbury different because of the racial makeup of the two communities, she wondered, or did it have more to do with the way she was teaching the novel?

OTHER STRATEGIES

Students engaged in several kinds of writing to help them understand the novel better. To help students understand the irony in *Huck Finn*, Jenkins asked them to list examples of irony from the text in their journals and share these in class (Exhibit D). She also gave them a list of ironic quotes to analyze in their journals. Jenkins followed a similar procedure with other literary techniques, such as satire.

She required students to write an essay by choosing a theme, showing how Twain develops it throughout the book, and drawing a conclusion about the author's purpose. First, the class brainstormed possible themes. Then Jenkins read them a sample essay that she had written on the theme of education in *Huck Finn*. She asked them to evaluate the essay and find any shortcomings. The students thought the essay was great, but Jenkins said she'd only give it a B, explaining that she needed to expand it by providing more specific details. Their task was to edit her essay to show where she needed to elaborate. Jenkins felt that it had been only fair for her to write her own essay first. "If I'm asking the students to do it, I should realize how hard the assignment actually is. Then, when it comes time for the students to write, they chuckle, 'Well, she's already done it, so I guess I can.'

"Sometimes they get frustrated with the time it takes for me to return their papers. I explain that they've spent considerable time composing their essays; it wouldn't be fair of me not to read them carefully. After reading them all once, I reread each paper. I return their quizzes the next day, but this takes about a week," Jenkins explained.

For a culminating activity, Jenkins wanted something special. Her only stipulation was that their projects creatively demonstrate their learning from the novel. They had to write a proposal for her to review.

MODIFICATIONS FOR STUDENTS WITH SPECIAL NEEDS

For the students with special needs, Jenkins tried several strategies. Often, these students needed written explanations as a complement or follow-up to oral discussions. She asked for volunteer scribes to summarize key ideas generated from group discussions and show them on the overhead projector. To ensure that students had accurate descriptions of their assignments, she handed out written directions or wrote the assignments on the chalkboard for students to copy.

When forming small groups, she divided the students with special needs among the groups. Then, if one had a hard time understanding something, a peer was available to explain. "When they're having difficulty, they seem to do better when peers give them an explanation than when I do," she said.

For help developing essays, four students received additional assistance either from the special education teacher or the teacher staffing the writing lab. In addition, Jenkins often paired students for peer editing. Each had to outline the partner's paper, using a graphic organizer to identify gaps. She found that if students worked with another person on the same theme, both developed new insights. Also, if students having difficulty with writing worked with a better writer, they had a model from whom to learn.

WHAT'S THE CONTROVERSY?

Since its banning at the Sandbury middle school and the ensuing conference at The Mark Twain House, *Huck Finn* continued to be prominently featured in the local and national news. Public radio hosted a talk show about teaching *Huck Finn*. Jane Smiley (1996), a Pulitzer Prize–winning novelist, published an article in *Harper's Magazine* accusing the novel of being racist, arguing that neither "Huck nor Twain takes Jim's desire for freedom at all seriously" (p. 63) and challenging the putative "greatness" of the novel's literary style. Twain biographer Justin Kaplan (1996) mounted a counterargument in the *New York Times Book Review*. It was perhaps no coincidence that a new edition of the novel, which included previously unpublished passages, was advertised in a special edition, "Black in America," in *The New Yorker* (Bradley, 1996).

Given the current controversy, Jenkins kept waiting for the other shoe to drop as she was teaching the novel. So far, very few of the concerns raised at the conference had surfaced in her classroom.

She had not seen signs of racism. She found the students occasionally making fun of the dialect, but they seemed to view these passages as southern dialect, not black dialect.

Generally, they did not react to the word "nigger". Jenkins had given them David Bradley's (1996) short article from *The New Yorker* in which he discussed the critical difference between the way Huck uses the word and the way Tom uses it.[1] When the class read the novel aloud, Jenkins permitted students to skip over the word "nigger" if they chose to. In most cases, they read it without seeming to pay much attention to it. Jenkins presumed this resulted from their discussion of Bradley's article. One student substituted the word *Negro*. Two other students seemed to skim ahead as they were reading and never volunteered to read a passage in which "nigger" appeared.

Jenkins discussed the students' perceptions of Jim. "The students have some trouble understanding Jim's dialect. They tend to view Jim like Huck in many ways. For example, they're both seeking their freedom, and they're both superstitious. I don't think the students see Jim as ignorant because he's black. We've compared Jim to Pap Finn and pointed out that Jim is a loving, truly concerned father figure. But they miss the idea that Jim is being treated unfairly by Huck. They think once Huck has stopped tricking Jim, Huck sees him as an equal.

"Perhaps we just haven't discussed this enough. I've been hesitant to discuss nineteenth-century racial theories of the inferiority of African Americans, for fear that I'd heighten misconceptions and offend, rather than clarifying the historical framework for my students. Maybe we haven't talked enough about the entire society being racist; I've tended to focus more broadly on human beings' inhumanity to each other. By the end, I want to show the growth in the way Huck sees Jim. Sometimes they gloss right over it. They're still literal minded. They're not looking deeply into the fact that one of the major ways Huck changes is in how he perceives his friend. I also want them to see how courageous Jim is."

Sandra, the one African-American student, was always in the back of Jenkins's mind. "I don't want to offend any of the kids. I certainly don't want to single Sandra out, yet I wonder whether she'll be upset by anything I say, such as my interpretation or way of explaining the racist attitudes in the novel. I want to be sure that I'm sensitive," Jenkins said.

"Sandra tends not to want to share," Jenkins continued. "When I asked the students a question about a racist episode in *To Kill a Mockingbird*, Sandra said, 'I don't know.' On the other hand, other kids gave the same response. I want Sandra's perspective to be that of just a child. I don't want her to feel she has to be the spokesperson for the African-American community. Though she's one of the three or four African-American kids in the school, I don't think the kids treat her any differently. Today, I found myself glancing at her when I said, 'Finally, Huck Finn is seeing Jim as a person. What was the problem before?' We related this to *To Kill a Mockingbird* in which Bob Ewell assumes that because he's white, he's a better person than Tom Robinson, the black man accused of rape. I was proud of the kids when they pointed out the irony that Bob's skin was probably just as dark as Tom's since he didn't wash. This is the one time I

---

[1] Bradley points out that Huck uses "nigger" to mean *Negro*, without negative connotations, whereas Tom uses it disparagingly. From reading *Huck Finn* as a child, Bradley began to learn the difference between connotation and denotation and to evaluate people's intent based in their actions, not their words.

heard the kids refer to the fact that Sandra is darker. A student who had just come back from a Florida vacation said to her, 'I've got darker skin than you.' 'No way,' said Sandra. 'I'll always be darker.'

"Sandra is a nice, popular kid who's full of the dickens. One of the brightest kids in the class, she's also one of the easiest to lose because she gets bored. When I think about it, I'm more worried about keeping her engaged than offending her. Also, I think Sandra is comfortable enough to approach me or to say something right out in class if she has a problem. I'm more concerned about upsetting another student who has been abused."

Summing up the classes' responses, Jenkins said, "The issue that people would assume would be most volatile—racism—hasn't been, perhaps because there's not much of a racial mix of students at the school. In retrospect, I might have used the journals to encourage more of a personal response, but that can be touchy, too."

Then she reflected further. "Making the book powerfully relevant to my students has had more to do with coming-of-age issues and concerns about child abuse and neglect than with racism, given the school community. I have to admit that I'm not as comfortable discussing racism as I had hoped I would be, and I'm only relieved that there hasn't been more controversy in the classroom or any criticism from parents. I've certainly tried to open the students' eyes to the problem of racism in the book, but should I have forced the issue? Does the responsible teacher *create* a controversy when teaching this book? I want to teach the book conscientiously, but I don't want to end up on page one of the newspapers like the teacher in Sandbury did."

OTHER CONCERNS

Jenkins found that student boredom was her greatest concern. The class was not moving through the book as quickly as expected. One reason was that she had fallen behind in the rereading she needed to do to keep on top of the details. She slowed the class's pace so she could keep abreast of the reading.

Also, as she stated, "I get caught up in all the things I want to share, yet I don't want to overteach. We've been working on this book for six weeks, and maybe we've beaten it to death. The hardest thing is dragging the kids through the reading. It's just tedious for them. Like the ebb and flow of the river, they speed up when the book gets exciting and slow down when it's less intriguing to them. It's ironic; when Huck and Jim are relaxing on the raft, they take a break themselves—during the more philosophical dialogues. I don't like to have to use the threat of a quiz to make them do the reading, but sometimes I have to."

To give students enough time to read, she provided digressions. For example, they made a chart comparing the social ills of the 1830s to the social ills of the 1990s. Then they discussed what an author's responsibility is to influence social issues and whether he or she can really effect change. "They just looked at me like I'd just grown a second head," she said. Then, to try to relate this to their lives, she asked whether they had ever read a book or seen a movie or TV show that had changed their thinking, "What kind of a reaction was Mark Twain trying to get from his readers?" she questioned her students. "We didn't get far, but it may have sparked some thought," she later commented. "I want to pull them into the text, to see how this relates to them, and I'm buying time to let them catch up on reading. They protest when I tell them too much of the story, but they're falling behind."

Sometimes, the kids themselves provided the digressions, seemingly to enliven the class. Jenkins felt a constant tension between letting the students take charge of the discussion and drawing them back to the text. "Sometimes I feel they're more interested in the connections to real life than the novel. After a discussion of the Duke and King's scams, they regaled each other with stories about con artists. Yet I don't know if that's wrong. If the intention of literature is to mirror life, isn't it important to connect the book to what they've seen? Don't I want them to come away with a new understanding of what's fair and what needs to be reformed in their own lives?"

FINISHING THE NOVEL

To quicken the pace, Jenkins decided to skip the last chapters, from Chapter 34 to the end, where Tom and Huck conspire to free Jim from the Phelps plantation. This was a first for her, but she felt it was necessary now. She summarized the remaining plot, and the class read aloud and discussed the ironic intent of key passages. Although it was not required, many students read the chapters on their own.

Jenkins decided to shorten the final test because of the many assignments on *Huck Finn* the students had completed already:

- Four essays
- Seven quizzes
- Several short projects
- Culminating project

In addition to the test, Jenkins gave the students Langston Hughes's poem "I Dream a World" and asked students to write a take-home essay comparing it to *Huck Finn* in terms of tone, theme, and the two authors' background and historical times. She also asked students to consider whether we, as a society, have moved forward in terms of eliminating racist attitudes and whether we still have a long way to go. After grading the tests, she was pleased with the results. There were some simple comparisons, such as that Hughes was African American and Twain was white, but also some more sophisticated responses. Several students thought that Hughes was more optimistic and foresaw the end of racism, whereas Twain was misanthropic and had far less confidence in the goodness of humankind.

The students presented their culminating projects after taking the test. Among them were four board games, model rafts, skits, several children's books based on scenes from the novel, and a gigantic papier-mâché model of the river. Jenkins felt that the projects were valuable in reinforcing certain ideas, such as what life on a raft might be like, and in providing an opportunity for those students who had difficulty comprehending the text to use their creativity.

FINAL REFLECTIONS

Summing up her feelings about the experience of teaching *Huck Finn*, Jenkins said, "It was pretty successful. For the most part, students enjoyed reading the book, and there are signs of continuing interest. Last week, we had a book fair, and I was delighted to see that at least ten kids bought copies of *Tom Sawyer* for summer reading.

"I don't think middle school is the only time *Huck Finn* could be taught or necessarily the best time. They'll take from it what they can and hopefully come back to it someday. A good novel is meant to be reread. There are always some unanswered questions.

"Every time I teach it," Jenkins continued, "I do it differently because I think there's something I forgot before or something that's more important that needs to be considered. Next time, I'd be better organized and try to stick to my time frame. I kept revising and adding things. I got really excited about the book and tried to do too much.

"For the very last activity, I gave the students a Twain quote, "Travel is fatal to prejudice, bigotry, and narrow-mindedness,' and asked them to answer the following questions in their journals:

1. How does this relate to what you know about Samuel Clemens?
2. How does this relate to *Huck Finn*?
3. How does this relate to your life and life in general?

"We had a lively discussion about the quote. One student said, 'If we're still traveling through life, at fourteen we haven't lost all our prejudices and ignorance. We need time to work our way through and to have more experiences to help us lose our prejudices.' Another student countered, 'Well, when you're this young, you haven't been able to develop prejudices. The more experiences you have, the more prejudiced you might become. My parents are more prejudiced than I am.'

"I don't think the theme of racism really hit them. They haven't had to deal with it personally. They were as upset or more by the way Pap Finn treated Huck and left him with little supervision. They could identify more with that.

"Their limited understanding is partially because of what they bring to the novel. Middle schoolers have had just so many experiences; hopefully, we'll take them a little beyond those."

Then, Jenkins paused. "It wouldn't matter whether I were teaching middle schoolers or not. I think this book would be much more challenging to teach in a racially diverse school district where kids have more direct experience with racism. I'd have to think about whether this might change the way I teach the book. How would I teach it if I were teaching in the city half an hour away?"

She paused again, recalling the stories she had heard of the Sandbury incident, as well as what she had read in the papers—how bitterly angry and pained for their children the African-American parents were and how unfairly attacked the white teacher felt. "Or would I even teach it?" Jenkins asked. "I wouldn't want to abandon teaching this book—I feel it has such merit. Yet would I willingly face that maelstrom?"

REFERENCES AND SELECTED BIBLIOGRAPHY

Bradley, D. (1996, June 26). That word. *The New Yorker*, p. 133.

Carey-Webb, A. (1993). Racism and Huckleberry Finn: Censorship, dialogue, and change. *English Journal*, 82(7), 22–34.

Chadwick-Joshua, J. (1991). Mark Twain and the fires of controversy: Teaching racially sensitive literature: Or, "Say that 'N' word and out you go!" In L. Champion (Ed.), *The critical response to Mark Twain's Huckleberry Finn* (pp. 228–237). Westport, CT: Greenwood.

Chadwick-Joshua, J. (1996, August 17). Pro & con: Should schools keep *Huck Finn* off the reading lists? No. Great books make us uncomfortable. *Hartford Courant*, p. A-10.

Champion, L. (1991). *The critical response to Mark Twain's Huckleberry Finn*. Westport, CT: Greenwood.

Fishkin, S. F. (1993). *Was Huck black? Mark Twain and African American voices*. New York: Oxford University Press.

Hughes, L. (1963). I dream a world. In A. Bontemps (Ed.), *American Negro poetry* (pp. 71–72). New York: Hill & Wang. (Originally published 1926.)

Kaplan, J. (1996, March 10). Selling *Huck Finn* down the river. *New York Times Book Review*, p. 27.

Leonard, J. S., Tenney, T. A., & Davis, T. M. (Eds.). (1992). *Satire or evasion? Black perspectives on Huckleberry Finn*. Durham, NC: Duke University Press.

Lew, A. (1993). Teaching Huck Finn in a multiethnic classroom. *English Journal*, 82(7), 16–21.

The Mark Twain House helps teachers teach *Adventures of Huckleberry Finn*. (1995, Fall). *Mark Twain News*, 3, 3–4.

Pierce, R. N. (1996, August 17). Pro & con: Should schools keep Huck Finn off the reading lists? Yes. The book is too sophisticated for teens. *Hartford Courant*, p. A-10.

Schuster, K. (1995, July 25). Teachers examine "Huck Finn." *New Haven Register*, pp. A3, A5.

Smiley, J. (1996, January). Say it ain't so, Huck. *Harper's Magazine*, pp. 61–67.

Wallace, J. H. (1992). The case against *Huck Finn*. In J. S. Leonard, T. A. Tenney, & T. M. Davis (Eds.), *Satire or evasion? Black perspective on Huckleberry Finn* (pp. 16–24). Durham, NC: Duke University Press.

EXHIBIT A

The Case Against Huck Finn[2]

John H. Wallace

The Issue

The *Adventures of Huckleberry Finn*, by Mark Twain, is the most grotesque example of racist trash ever written. During the 1981–82 school year, the media carried reports that it was challenged in Davenport, Iowa; Houston, Texas; Bucks County, Pennsylvania; and, of all places, Mark Twain Intermediate School in Fairfax County, Virginia. Parents in Waukegan, Illinois, in 1983 and in Springfield, Illinois, in 1984 asked that the book be removed from the classroom—and there are many challenges to this book that go unnoticed by the press. All of these are coming from black parents and teachers after complaints from their children or students, and frequently they are supported by white teachers, as in the case of Mark Twain Intermediate School.

For the past forty years, black families have trekked to schools in numerous districts throughout the country to say, "This book is a classic." Classic or not, it should not be allowed to continue to cause our children embarrassment about their heritage.

Louisa May Alcott, the Concord Public Library, and others condemned the book as trash when it was published in 1885. The NAACP and the National Urban League successfully collaborated to have *Huckleberry Finn* removed from the classrooms of the public schools of New York City in 1957 because it uses the term "nigger." In 1969 Miami-Dade Junior College removed the book from its classrooms because the administration believed that the book creates an emotional block for black students that inhibits learning. It was excluded from the classrooms of the New Trier High School in Winnetka, Illinois, and removed from the required reading list in the state of Illinois in 1976.

My own research indicates that the assignment and reading aloud of *Huckleberry Finn* in our classrooms is humiliating and insulting to black students. It contributes to their feelings of low self-esteem and to the white students' disrespect for black people. It constitutes mental cruelty, harassment, and outright racial intimidation to force black students to sit in the classroom with their white peers and read *Huckleberry Finn*. The attitudes developed by the reading of such literature can lead to tensions, discontent, and even fighting. If this book is removed from the required reading lists of our schools, there should be improved student-to-student, student-to-teacher, and teacher-to-teacher relationships.

---

[2]From *Satire or Evasion? Black Perspectives on Huckleberry Finn* (pp. 16–24) by James S. Leonard, Thomas A. Tenney, and Thadious M. Davis (Eds.). Copyright 1992, Duke University Press. Reprinted with permission.

"Nigger"

According to *Webster's Dictionary*, the word "nigger" means a Negro or a member of any dark-skinned race of people and is *offensive*. Black people have never accepted "nigger" as a proper term—not in George Washington's time, Mark Twain's time, nor William Faulkner's time. A few white authors, thriving on making blacks objects of ridicule and scorn by having blacks use this word as they, the white authors, were writing and speaking for blacks in a dialect they perceived to be peculiar to black people, may have given the impression that blacks accepted the term. Nothing could be further from the truth.

Some black authors have used "nigger," but not in literature to be consumed by children in the classroom. Black authors know as well as whites that there is money to be made selling books that ridicule black people. As a matter of fact, the white child learns early in life that his or her black peer makes a good butt for a joke. Much of what goes on in the classroom reinforces this behavior. Often the last word uttered before a fight is "nigger." Educators must discourage the ridicule of "different" children.

In the Classroom

Russell Baker, of *The New York Times* (14 April 1982), has said (and Jonathan Yardley, of the *Washington Post* [10 May 1982], concurred):

> Kids are often exposed to books long before they are ready for them or exposed to them in a manner that seems almost calculated to evaporate whatever enthusiasm the students may bring to them. . . . Very few youngsters of high school age are ready for *Huckleberry Finn*. Leaving aside its subtle depiction of racial attitudes and its complex view of American society, the book is written in a language that will seem baroque, obscure and antiquated to many young people today. The vastly sunnier *Tom Sawyer* is a book for kids, but *Huckleberry Finn most emphatically is not*.

The milieu of the classroom is highly charged with emotions. There are twenty to thirty unique personalities with hundreds of needs to be met simultaneously. Each student wants to be accepted and to be like the white, middle-class child whom he perceives to be favored by the teacher. Since students do not want their differences highlighted, it is best to accentuate their similarities; but the reading of *Huck Finn* in class accentuates the one difference that is always apparent—color.

My research suggests that the black child is offended by the use of the word "nigger" anywhere, no matter what rationale the teacher may use to justify it. If the teacher permits its use, the black child tends to reject the teacher because the student is confident that the teacher is prejudiced. Communications are effectively severed, thwarting the child's education. Pejorative terms should not be granted any legitimacy by their use in the classroom under the guise of teaching books of great literary merit, nor for any other reason.

Equal Protection and Opportunity in the Classroom

To paraphrase Irwin Katz, the use of the word "nigger" by a prestigious adult like a teacher poses a strong *social* threat to the black child. Any expression by a white or black teacher of dislike or devaluation, whether through harsh, indifferent, or patronizing behavior, would tend to have an unfavorable effect on the performance of black children in their school work. This is so because *various psychological theories suggest that the black students' covert reactions to the social threat would constitute an important source of intellectual impairment.*

Dorothy Gilliam, writing in the *Washington Post* (12 April 1982), said, "First Amendment rights are crucial to a healthy society. No less crucial is the Fourteenth Amendment and its guarantee of equal protection under the law." *The use of the word "nigger" in the classroom does not provide black students with equal protection and is in violation of their constitutional rights. Without equal protection, they have neither equal access nor equal opportunity for an education.*

One group of citizens deeply committed to effecting change and to retaining certain religious beliefs sacred to themselves are members of the Jewish religion. In a publication issued by the Jewish Community Council (November 1981), the following guidelines were enunciated regarding the role of religious practices in public schools: "In no event should any student, teacher, or public school staff member feel that his or her own beliefs or practices are being questioned, infringed upon, or compromised by programs taking place in or sponsored by the public school." Further, "schools should avoid practices which operate to single out and isolate 'different' pupils and thereby [cause] embarrassment."

I endorse these statements without reservation, for I believe the rationale of the Jewish Community Council is consistent with my position. I find it incongruent to contend that it is fitting and proper to shelter children from isolation, embarrassment, and ridicule due to their religious beliefs and then deny the same protection to other children because of the color of their skin. The basic issue is the same. It is our purpose to spare children from scorn, to increase personal pride, and to foster the American belief of acceptance on merit, not color, sex, religion, or origin.

The Teacher

Many "authorities" say *Huckleberry Finn* can be used in our intermediate and high school classrooms. They consistently put stipulations on its use like the following: It must be used with appropriate planning. It is the responsibility of the teacher to assist students in the understanding of the historical setting of the novel, the characters being depicted, the social context, including prejudice, which existed at the time depicted in the book. Balanced judgment on the part of the classroom teacher must be used prior to making a decision to utilize this book in an intermediate or high school program. Such judgment would include taking into account the age and maturity of the student, their ability to comprehend abstract concepts, and the methodology of presentation.

Any material that requires such conditions could be dangerous racist propaganda in the hands of even our best teachers. And "some, not all, teachers are hostile, racist, vindictive, inept, or even neurotic," though "many are compassionate and skillful." Teacher attitudes are important to students. Some teachers are marginal at best, yet many school administrators are willing to trust them with a book that maligns blacks. H*uckleberry Finn* would have been out of the classroom ages ago if it used "dago," "wop," or "spic."

When "authorities" mention the "historical setting" of H*uckleberry Finn*, they suggest that it is an accurate, factual portrayal of the way things were in slavery days. In fact, the book is the outgrowth of Mark Twain's memory and imagination, written twenty years after the end of slavery. Of the two main characters depicted, one is a thief, a liar, a sacrilegious corn-cob-pipe-smoking truant; the other is a self-deprecating slave. No one would want his children to emulate this pair. Yet some "authorities" speak of Huck as a boyhood hero. Twain warns us in the beginning of H*uckleberry Finn*, "Persons attempting to find a motive in this narrative will be prosecuted; persons attempting to find a moral in it will be banished; persons attempting to find a plot in it will be shot." I think we ought to listen to Twain and stop feeding this trash to our children. It does absolutely nothing to enhance racial harmony. The prejudice that existed then is still very much apparent today. Racism against blacks is deeply rooted in the American culture and is continually reinforced by the schools, by concern for socioeconomic gain, and by the vicarious ego enhancement it brings to those who manifest it.

H*uckleberry Finn* is racist, whether its author intended it to be or not. The book implies that black people are not honest. For example, Huck says about Jim: "It most froze me to hear such talk. He wouldn't ever dared to talk such talk in his life before. Just see what a difference it made in him the minute he judged he was about free. It was according to the old saying, 'give a nigger an inch and he'll take an ell.' Thinks I, this is what comes of my not thinking" (chap. 16). And in another section of the book, the Duke, in reply to a question from the King, says: "Mary Jane'll be in mourning from this out; and the first you know the nigger that does up the rooms will get an order to box these duds up and put 'em away; and do you reckon a nigger can run across money and not borrow some of it?" (chap. 26).

H*uckleberry Finn* also insinuates that black people are less intelligent than whites. In a passage where Huck and Tom are trying to get the chains off Jim, Tom says: "They couldn't get the chain off, so they just cut their hand off and shoved. And a leg would be better still. But we got to let that go. There ain't necessity enough in this case; and, besides, Jim's a nigger, and wouldn't understand the reason for it" (chap. 35). On another occasion, when Tom and Huck are making plans to get Jim out of the barn where he is held captive, Huck says: "He told him everything. Jim, he couldn't see no sense in most of it, but he allowed we was white folks and knowed better than him; so he was satisfied, and said he would do it all just as Tom said" (chap. 36).

Twain said in H*uckleberry Finn*, more than 100 years ago, what Dr. W. B. Shockley and A. R. Jensen are trying to prove through empirical study today. This tells us something about the power of the printed word when it is taught to children by a formidable institution such as the school.

Huckleberry Finn even suggests that blacks are not human beings. When Huck arrives at Aunt Sally's house, she asks him why he is late:

"We blowed a cylinder head."
"Good gracious! Anybody hurt?"
"No'm. Killed a nigger."
"Well, it's lucky; because sometimes people do get hurt." (Ch. 32)

There are indications that the racist views and attitudes implicit in the preceding quotations are as prevalent in America today as they were more than 100 years ago. *Huckleberry Finn* has not been successful in fighting race hate and prejudice, as its proponents maintain, but has helped to retain the status quo.

The Black Student

In 1963 John Fisher, former president of Columbia Teachers College, stated:

The black American youngster happens to be a member of a large and distinctive group that for a very long time has been the object of special political, legal, and social action. . . . To act as though any child is separable from his history is indefensible. In terms of educational planning, it is *irresponsible*.

Every black child is the victim of the history of his race in this country. On the day he enters kindergarten, he carries a burden *no white child* can ever know, no matter what other handicaps or disabilities he may suffer.

The primary school child learns, almost the minute he enters school, that black is associated with dirtiness, ugliness, and wickedness. Much of what teachers and students think of the black child is color based. As a result, the black pupil knows his pigmentation is an impediment to his progress.

As early as the fifth grade, the black student studies U.S. history and must accept his ancestors in the role of slaves. This frustrating and painful experience leaves scars that very few educators, writers, and especially English teachers can understand. We compound these problems for black children when we force them to read aloud the message of *Huckleberry Finn*. It is so devastatingly traumatic that the student may never recover. How much pain must a black child endure to secure an education? No other child is asked to suffer so much embarrassment, humiliation, and racial intimidation at the hands of so powerful an institution as the school. The vast majority of black students have no tolerance for either "ironic" or "satirical" postslavery times.

Dorothy Gilliam (*Washington Post*, 12 April 1982) makes a good case for protecting the rights of students when she says, "Where rights conflict, one must sometimes supersede the other. Freedom of speech does not, for example, allow words to be deliberately used in a way that would cause someone to suffer a heart attack. By the same token, the use of words in ways that cause psychological and emotional damage is an unacceptable exercise of free speech."

Racism

If indeed, as *Huckleberry Finn*'s proponents claim, the book gives a positive view of blacks and has an antislavery, antiracist message, then the Nazi party, the Ku Klux Klan, and the White Citizens Council must see something different. Most of the hate mail received when a school in northern Virginia restricted the use of the book was from these groups.

It is difficult to believe that Samuel Clemens would write a book against the institution of slavery; he did, after all, join a Confederate army bent on preserving that peculiar institution. Also, he could not allow Huck to help Jim to his freedom. It seems he was a hodgepodge of contradictions.

Huckleberry Finn is an American classic for no other reason than that it ridicules blacks to a greater extent than any other book given children to read. The book and racism feed on each other and have withstood the test of time because many Americans insist on preserving our racist heritage.

Marguerite Barnett (1982) points out:

> By ridiculing blacks, exaggerating their facial features, and denying their humanity, the popular art of the Post-Civil-War period represented the political culture's attempt to deny blacks the equal status and rights awarded them in the Emancipation Proclamation. By making blacks inhuman, American whites could destroy their claim to equal treatment. Blacks as slaves posed no problem because they were under complete domination, but blacks as free men created political problems. The popular culture of the day supplied the answer by dehumanizing blacks and picturing them as childlike and inferior.

In this day of enlightenment, teachers should not rely on a book that teaches the subtle sickness of racism to our young and causes so much psychological damage to a large segment of our population. We are a multicultural, pluralistic nation. We must teach our young to respect all races, ethnic groups, and religious groups in most positive terms conceivable.

Recommendations

This book should not be used with children. It is permissible to use the original *Huckleberry Finn* with students in graduate courses of history, English, and social science if one wants to study the perpetration and perpetuation of racism. The caustic, abrasive language is less likely to offend students of that age group because they tend to be mature enough to understand and discuss issues without feeling intimidated by the instructor, fellow students, or racism.

EXHIBIT B

Pro and Con: Should Schools Keep *Huck Finn* Off Reading Lists?[3]

No. Great Books Make Us Uncomfortable
Jocelyn Chadwick-Joshua[4]

Mark Twain's *Adventures of Huckleberry Finn* represents more than just a canonical space-holder for the late 19th century. It represents a realistic, rather than romantic rendering of the antebellum American South and the ambivalent post-Reconstruction North.

Is such a work comfortable reading? Most decidedly not, but then are *The Iliad*, *Othello*, *The Merchant of Venice*? Are any of these works ever taught without careful guidance and preparation by the teacher? I sincerely hope not. I have yet to meet the student who needs no guidance for any piece of literature.

Twain's use of "nigger" and "poor white trash" are uncomfortable terms used deliberately to allow the reader to experience what characters Jim, Huck, plantation slaves, and others in the book feel. Nineteenth-century African-American writers who chose the American South as their focal point often used the same terminology to make their points. Do we ban them, too?

Adventures of Huckleberry Finn is not racist. What Twain accomplishes in this novel is to immerse the Northern and Southern audience into the (re)thinking and (re)imagining of the African American in this country. Who better for such a task than one who was reared in the slave-holding South, whose family had slaves and who came to the issue with one idea firmly established and then changes that idea when the facts do not match with what he had previously learned?

We observe Huck Finn in this identical dilemma: An adolescent boy who believes what he has been told by "trustworthy" people is put in a traumatic and disillusioning position when he is confronted by a different truth.

So why is this novel consistently on the list of banned books across this country? It seeks to agitate and succeeds in agitating. Huck and Jim invade the comfort of our private spaces and compel us to listen to and observe what is being said and who is saying it; what is being done and who is doing it. It takes the modern reader into the life of a slave of the South and, more important, into the mind and motivation of a slave.

---

[3] From *The Hartford Courant*: (Saturday Commentary) Saturday, August 17, 1996, p. A-10. Reprinted by permission.

[4] Jocelyn Chadwick–Joshua is associate director of the Teachers Academy at the Dallas Institute of Humanities & Cultures.

So, do we ban this book? I ask, do we ban the Confederate flag? So we ban the Bible or the Koran or the Pentateuch? Literature provides for the mind a safe window from which we can observe how other people who resemble ourselves respond to situations and problems and truths.

Through this literature we begin to understand more clearly Huck Finn's evolving understanding of Jim and his race as equal, human individuals. Huck's recognition is one that because of what he has been taught all his life somehow "don't seem natural, but I reckon it's so"—that Southern slaves have feelings and emotional and filial relationships just as their white Southern counterparts.

Banning *Adventures of Huckleberry Finn* from school curriculums is submerging texts that can aid us in never forgetting from where we have all come, how we came to be here, and where we go from here.

Yes. The Book Is Too Sophisticated for Teens
Richard N. Pierce[5]

Although I have given my honors-level 12th-graders the option of reading "Adventures of Huckleberry Finn," I don't think the novel is appropriate for general use in grades 7 through 12. The very fact that "one of the greatest anti-racist works of fiction ever written," as Twain scholar Shelley Fisher Fishkin called it, has been accused of racism suggests that there's more to the work than might appear on the surface.

First of all, the novel is subtly satirical in its nature. Satire, relying on irony to expose human foolishness and corruption, is easily misunderstood. The ability to recognize irony is said to be one of the surest tests of intelligence and sophistication, for the reader has to understand that the intended meaning is the opposite of the expressed meaning.

When, for example, in Chapter 19 Huck and Jim hear the duke's story about how far he's fallen in life, Huck says, "Jim pitied him ever so much, and so did I." By this time, however, we readers, if we are discerning, feel no pity because we realize the duke is a fraud, a fact not clear to Huck for a long time.

It is the satirical tone of the work that takes the edge off the word "nigger," which is offensive to many. Since the whole novel ridicules a society that cleaves to racist institutions, "nigger," every time it's used, punctuates the story with critical barbs against racism. The height of the struggle comes in Chapter 31 with Huck's exclamation, as he decides to help Jim go free: "All right, then, I'll *go* to hell."

Huck's very conscience has been constituted by a society in which religion and law conspired to enslave human beings. He may not understand that his decision is right and noble, but we readers, if we are discerning, surely do.

---

[5]Richard N. Pierce retired from Hartford's Weaver High School English faculty in 1994. He teaches writing at the University of Hartford's College of Arts and Sciences.

. And if the subtle satire isn't enough to thwart young readers' understanding of Twain's novel, there is also the fact that it stands at the juncture between two major schools of American literature—romanticism and realism, which themselves add a depth of meaning to the story.

Romanticism, which was fading fast after the Civil War, emphasized imagination and heroic adventure. Realism, by contrast, was obsessed with the everyday life of the average person. The two ideologies face off during the last quarter of the novel. In Chapter 33, when Huck meets Tom on the road to Aunt Sally's, he confides in Tom that he is trying to steal Jim out of slavery. Tom almost blurts out the news that Jim has already been freed by Miss Watson's will, but he first stops and thinks. Then "his eye lit up" and he said," I'll *help* you steal him!" In Chapter 42, when asked why he did it, Tom says, "I wanted the *adventure* of it." For Huck, the realist, stealing Jim had been a wrenching decision and desperate struggle; but to Tom, the romanticist, it was all a make-believe adventure.

Adventures of Huckleberry Finn is appropriate for older teens and adults, but most younger people haven't attained the intellectual maturity needed to interpret the satire or to understand Twain's espousal of realism. Let's be fair and teach the novel to those who can best understand it.

EXHIBIT C

Adventures of Huckleberry Finn Plot Summary

In *Adventures of Huckleberry Finn*, Huck, an adolescent growing up along the Mississippi River in the 1840s, tells his own story. The son of the town drunkard, he has been abandoned by his father and virtually adopted by the Widow Douglas and her sister, Miss Watson. Huck is prone to drinking and swearing. He resists their restrictions and resents being sent to school to learn to read and write. He slowly begins to adjust when his abusive father returns to claim him and, not coincidentally, a fortune recently found by Huck and his friend, Tom Sawyer. Anticipating his father's greedy motive, Huck signs the fortune over to a local judge to prevent his father from acquiring it.

Nevertheless, Huck's father takes his son from the Widow Douglas to a cabin in the woods, where he keeps the boy prisoner and brutally beats him. Desperate to get away, Huck escapes, faking his own death to avoid being recaptured. While in hiding on a nearby island, Huck discovers Jim, Miss Watson's slave. Jim had run away, fearing that he would be sold to a new owner.

Huck and Jim decide to flee downriver on a raft. Among their many adventures, they encounter two con artists, the Duke and the King, with whom they travel for some time. Stricken by his conscience, Huck ultimately exposes the two as frauds. The Duke and the King escape, however, and rejoin Huck and Jim. Later, the Duke sells Jim to Silas Phelps for ransom money. Huck is torn between what he believes is an obligation to return a slave to his original owner, Miss Watson, and his feelings of loyalty and love for Jim. He decides he is willing to "go to hell" for Jim and will help him escape from the Phelps' plantation.

At the Phelps' plantation, Huck is mistaken for Tom Sawyer, the Phelps' nephew. When Tom himself arrives, he assumes a different identity and plays along with Huck's ruse. To Huck's surprise, Tom agrees to help set Jim free—but only if they stage an elaborate escape, like an adventure story. Jim continues to suffer while Tom carries out his ridiculous scheme. When Jim finally escapes, Tom is shot in the leg during the ensuing chase. Despite his mistreatment, Jim sacrifices his opportunity for freedom to nurse Tom while Huck goes for the doctor. Later, Tom reveals that Miss Watson had died two months earlier and in her will had set Jim free already. Soon, Tom's Aunt Polly arrives and exposes the true identities of the two boys. When Jim reveals that he had seen Huck's father dead floating down the river, Huck decides to head for new territory to avoid being adopted and "sivilized" by Aunt Sally.

EXHIBIT D

Journal Activities

Questions

1. Respond to (one of) these questions in your binder. Please date your entry (entries).
2. What is your initial response to the reading?
3. What did you like or dislike about the reading?
4. Formulate a question based on the text. Answer that question.
5. While you were reading, what surprised you, made you think or upset you?
6. Name two details in the text which you consider important. Explain their importance.
7. List any new learning or appreciation which occurred during the reading of the text.
8. What about the text would you like to know or talk more about?
9. Does anything in your reading (character, setting, plot . . .) remind you of another piece of literature, movie, opera, TV show, etc.?

Irony Assignment

All of the following quotations illustrate Mark Twain's masterful use of *irony*.

Directions

In your journal, answer the following questions for each quotation:

- Who is speaking?
- What has just happened or is now happening at this point in the novel?
- Why is this quotation an example of *irony*?

1. Persons attempting to find a motive in this narrative will be prosecuted; persons attempting to find a moral in it will be banished; persons attempting to find a plot in it will be shot. (p. 10)
2. I did wish Tom Sawyer was there; I knowed he would take an interest in this kind of business, and throw in the fancy touches. (p. 41)
3. If they'd 'a' had some bullets in, I reckon they'd 'a' got the corpse they was after. (p. 46)
4. Yes; en I's rich now, come to look at it. I owns myself, en I's wuth eight hund'd dollars. (p. 54)

5. I'm unfavorable to killin' a man as long as you can git aroun' it; it ain't good sense, it ain't good morals. (p. 74)
6. It was fifteen minutes before I could work myself up to go and humble myself to a nigger; but I done it, and I warn't ever sorry for it afterward, neither. (p. 99)
7. Dah you goes, de ole true Huck; de on'y white gentleman dat ever kep' his promise to ole Jim. (p. 92)
8. . . . what's the use you learning to do right when it's troublesome to do right and ain't no trouble to do wrong, and the wages is jus the same? . . . after this always do whichever comes handiest at the time. (pp. 94–95)
9. I was powerful glad to get away from the feuds . . . there warn't no home like a raft . . . other places do seem so cramped up and smothery, but a raft don't. You feel mighty free and easy and comfortable on a raft. (p. 117)
10. . . . here am I, forlorn, torn from my high estate, hunted of men . . . degraded to the companionship of felons on a raft. (p. 123)
11. Set down, my boy; I wouldn't strain myself if I was you. I reckon you ain't used to lying, it don't seem to come handy; what you want is practice. You do it pretty awkward. (p. 193)
12. All right, then I'll *go* to hell. (p. 207)

EXHIBIT E

Persuasive Speech Activity

For the student presentations, Jenkins had written note-taking guidelines on the chalkboard:

Orator:
Quotes and/or comments:

After reviewing her guidelines, she asked for a volunteer to begin the speeches. She advised the other students, "Invoke your great listening skills and practice your note taking. Within Jamie's first paragraph, you should be able to determine right away what she proposes." Jamie delivered a long, eloquent speech, full of vivid details from the novel.

When she finished, the class broke into spontaneous applause. With her usual supportive tone, Jenkins asked, "How about some comments?" After several student responses, Jenkins summarized, "Jamie did a fine job of considering the social, educational, and psychological aspects of Huck being with each of the possible guardians. She elaborated on each, using good examples from the book. Remember when we read *To Kill a Mockingbird*? Jamie was our child psychologist then. She shows the same concerns about Huck."

Next, Nathan gave his speech, emphasizing the importance of Huck receiving adequate physical care, psychological support, and educational opportunities. He concluded, "Don't let biological ties waver your instincts" and then rushed to get out of the limelight. "Stay right here," Jenkins cajoled. Turning to the class, she asked, "What persuasive techniques did Nathan use?" They pointed out his strong conclusion and appeal to emotions. Jenkins added that he had asked rhetorical questions, such as, "Don't we want to break the cycle of abuse?"

Then it was Jesse's turn. After his rousing speech, the students gave feedback and Jenkins summarized. "Jesse used a couple of great strategies. 'If Huck stays with his father, he'll become his father,' he said. Showing cause and effect is an excellent persuasive tool."

Melissa began her speech by asking, "Gentlemen, how many of you think that education is important? Well, I certainly do. Huck Finn has the opportunity to get an education at the Widow Douglas's house." She concluded by stating, "The Widow Douglas wants a child to love and care for while Mr. Finn just wants another drink." Jenkins's class pointed out that Melissa had effectively used the technique of comparison and contrast, highlighting the differences between the Widow Douglas and Huck's father.

DISCUSSION QUESTIONS

1. How did attending the conference at The Mark Twain House affect Jenkins's teaching of *Huck Finn*?
2. Identify and evaluate Jenkins's teaching strategies.
   - How effectively does Jenkins promote critical thinking?
   - How effectively does she encourage the development of writing skills?
   - How effectively does she create instructional opportunities that are adapted to diverse learners?
   - How effectively do the activities and projects foster students' deep understanding of the novel?
3. What other teaching materials or strategies might Jenkins have used?
   - If Jenkins and other faculty on her team wanted to implement a more interdisciplinary approach to teaching *Huck Finn*, what would you recommend?
   - Do you agree with Jenkins's decision to skip the last chapters? Why or why not?
   - After reviewing Exhibit E, what kind of preliminary activity or pre-teaching would you do for the persuasive speech activity?
4. Jenkins comments that "the intention of literature is to mirror life" and tries to make the novel relevant to her students' lives. Do we overemphasize "relevance" in schools? Why not approach the novel historically and use it to help students understand people and places unconnected to them?
   - Jenkins skipped providing more of an historical background to the novel because students were eager to begin reading. Was it wise to let students follow their interests? Why or why not?
   - How can students ever appreciate the concept of history if they spend all of their time bringing everything back to themselves? Can they understand literature that is set in a certain historical period if they do not have knowledge of that period? For example, *Huck Finn* is set in the 1840s, before the Civil War, when fugitive slave laws were in effect. Runaway slaves who were caught were subject to brutal punishment, such as whipping and maiming. Those who aided a slave's escape were penalized. Twain wrote *Huck Finn* during the 1870s and 1880s, when Jim Crow laws made racial segregation legal in many parts of the South. Do students need this type of background knowledge to determine the motivations of the main characters as well as Twain's intent in writing the novel? Or should "great" literature stand on its own, independent of context?
   - How might an American Studies teacher approach teaching *Huck Finn*?
5. Although Jenkins referred to the controversial aspects of *Huck Finn*, she adopted the stance that the novel is not racist. What do you think about that?
   - From a pedagogical point of view: Are middle schoolers capable of evaluating the opposing positions?
   - From an ethical point of view: The information Jenkins chose to share from the summer conference documented only one side of this controversial issue. Was that appropriate?
   - If you were teaching the novel, would you share, for example, John Wallace's article (Exhibit A), which condemns the book as racist? Why or why not?

6. Consider further the issues in teaching racially sensitive literature.
    - Do you think it is possible that Jenkins has misread Sandra's responses to *Huck Finn*?
    - Was Jenkins singling out Sandra by bending over backwards not to single her out?
    - Should Jenkins have asked Sandra more directly for her contributions? Might both Sandra and the other students have benefited from hearing and discussing Sandra's perspectives on *Huck Finn* and racism?
    - The superintendent of the Sandbury middle school decided to ban *Huck Finn* from the middle school curriculum. Considering the arguments that were presented in this case, do you agree with his decision?
    - Consider the question Jenkins asks herself at the end of the case: should she teach the book any differently if she were teaching it in a racially diverse school? Why or why not? If so, how?
    - If Jenkins were teaching *Huck Finn* in a racially diverse school, what might be possible parental concerns, and how should she address these?
7. In a field such as English, where experts might compose a canon, or list of "must reads," how do responsible professionals determine what should be on the list?
    - What criteria should be used to identify which "classics" should stay on the list and which should go?
8. Do you think middle schoolers in general are intellectually and emotionally mature enough to read *Huck Finn*?
    - Is it developmentally appropriate? Give specific evidence from the case to support your position. What were Jenkins's successes in teaching the novel? Problems?
9. Discuss how similar controversies could occur in other disciplines, and give specific examples. (This question may be explored in greater depth by having students break into groups by subject matter areas.)

CASE 5

Discussion Question	Corresponding INTASC Principle
2	**7** The teacher plans instruction based upon knowledge of subject matter, students, the community, and curriculum goals.
	9 The teacher is a reflective practitioner who continually evaluates the effects of his/her choices and actions on others (students, parents, and other professionals in the learning community) and who actively seeks out opportunities to grow professionally.
3	**3** The teacher understands how students differ in their approaches to learning and creates instructional opportunities that are adapted to diverse learners.
	6 The teacher uses knowledge of effective verbal, nonverbal, and media communication techniques to foster active inquiry, collaboration, and supportive instruction in the classroom.
4, 8	**2** The teacher understands how children learn and develop, and can provide learning opportunities that support their intellectual, social and personal development.
5	**4** The teacher understands and uses a variety of instructional strategies to encourage students' development of critical thinking, problem solving, and performance skills.
9	**1** The teacher understands the concepts, tools of inquiry, and the structures of the discipline(s) he or she teaches and can create learning experiences that make these aspects of subject matter meaningful for students.

CASE SIX

On the High Wire

IN THE LOUNGE

"OK, let's talk," began Betsy Rogers, the team leader, as she looked around the table at the other three members of her team. Ignoring the spring foliage and bright sunshine outside a nearby window, the three averted their eyes as Rogers continued. "We've never hesitated to tell each other how we feel before. You obviously don't seem altogether comfortable with this unit. Why?"

"I'll start," said David Campbell, a tenth-year teacher. "I have mixed feelings. You all know me. I'm used to being in front of the class more—even the kids ask when I'll start teaching again. I've become much more comfortable with cooperative learning during the past few years of reform, but my strength is in presenting material in an interesting and fun way—I think I've learned how to be effective doing that. With this unit, I stand around watching kids work. It's difficult not to control the decisions students make—but I admit they like it and are learning. The bottom line with this unit is that I feel like my teaching strengths have lost purpose."

Darlene Wood, in whom Rogers took a special interest because of her status as a new teacher, nodded in agreement. "I can relate to that. Even though I'm still learning what works best for me, I know I thrive on organization. Planning is one of my strong points, and during this unit I haven't been able to do much of that. I'm just not very comfortable in an unstructured environment, even though I felt better after we discussed strategies for facilitating student planning. Everything I've learned has encouraged me to be reform minded, and I can't argue with what I've seen—fewer discipline problems and students effectively leading and participating in groups. Still, even with my limited experience I think I have a better idea of quality learning experiences than most eleven-year-olds!"

"I have another concern," Nina Scott, a fourth-year science teacher, interjected as she shifted in her chair. "I'm concerned that we didn't generate enough grades this six weeks because of this unit. The fact that it is not graded has raised some eyebrows, and understandably so. I hope parents will understand that we will 'assess' the unit without grading it. Also, some students are not contributing much to their groups' efforts, and I don't think there is enough accountability to encourage them to make a serious contribution."

They all looked expectantly at Rogers. Because her team members were known for their flexibility and willingness to implement reform initiatives, she had felt certain they would welcome the opportunity to pilot a student-generated unit and that they would adjust quickly. Despite her continued enthusiasm for the concept, Rogers knew that her team's practical concerns would have to be addressed.

THE SCHOOL

Built in the late 1940s as the town high school, Wakefield Middle School was large and imposing. The interior was notable for its high ceilings and tall windows that framed the picturesque lawn surrounding the school. The halls were covered with worn gray carpet that suggested years of disrepair. A major renovation was taking place in planned increments. A few examples of student work adorned the interior of the school, but for the most part the walls remained an unrelenting off-white with one exception: a hand-painted stripe design in the school colors bordered the entrance stairwells.

The school was located at the center of Wakefield, a small town that served as a bedroom community for a large urban area nearby; recent and rapid economic expansion promoted new business opportunities and several housing developments in Wakefield. As a result of this growth, a majority of Wakefield students came from predominantly middle-class families.

The school had thirty-five faculty members in grades six, seven, and eight and an enrollment of approximately seven hundred students. Until recently, the school grouped students primarily through departmentalization and some tracking. With the passage of statewide reform and the arrival of a new principal, however, a number of innovations took place. The overall result at Wakefield was the establishment of a permanent team system. Each team consisted of four teachers, one from each of the following disciplines: math, science, language arts, and social studies. The sixth grade had two teams, and there was one team in both the seventh and eighth grades. The other grouping consisted of a seventh-/eighth-grade combination team.

Living in a prosperous community close to a large city, Wakefield students had many cultural advantages children in more rural areas of the state did not. Most students experienced award-winning theater, ballet, museums, and other types of school field trips designed to build background knowledge. Many of the students went on family vacations to coastal areas or other geographically diverse locations, attended area concerts, or regularly participated in family hobbies such as hunting, shooting competitions, or water sports. Activities such as intramural sports, dance classes, Scouts, and church activities kept many students involved and occupied after school.

TEAM LEADER

Betsy Rogers was a dynamic, thirty-nine-year-old teacher who was recently named Middle School Teacher of the Year. Her style of dress, like her manner, was professional without being overly formal. Her intense energy and insistence that students think for themselves were evident in all aspects of her teaching.

Rogers sought to put into practice the innovative concepts that she learned during her education and training at a small liberal arts college. "Open classrooms," "students choice," and "learning centers" were still common catchwords when she graduated in the early 1980s. Moreover, her student teaching experience involved team-teaching second grade with another student teacher in an open classroom—a fairly unique assignment.

Rogers spent her first eight years teaching as the only fifth-grade teacher in a small mountain community. There, she frequently organized her teaching around the concept of student choice, emphasizing student contracts and learning centers. During this time she sought out training in Junior Great Books discussions and in the writing process approach, which she added to her repertoire. Her success with effective and innovative teaching strategies attracted the attention of a local university; Rogers began teaching a reading and language arts methods course during the summer months and continued in this adjunct role for several years.

The importance of these early experiences to Rogers' professional development became a topic of conversations with Darlene Wood. Rogers took an active interest in encouraging her younger colleague's involvement in innovative teaching strategies by reflecting on her own successes and dilemmas and their relevance at Wakefield. As a language arts teacher at several grade levels, Rogers stayed current with research in middle school philosophy, reading and writing methods, and national reform.

TEAM TEACHERS

The other members of Rogers' interdisciplinary sixth-grade team brought varied experiences and perspectives to the collaboration. Scott, Campbell, and Rogers taught together for two years before being joined by Wood at the beginning of last year.

Having just completed a master's degree, Nina Scott was knowledgeable in middle school concepts and philosophy. In her science classroom, she focused on concrete applications of principles and promoted the effective use of collaborative learning. For this reason, she placed great importance on her own demonstration lessons; she often gave open-note tests and quizzes to check for understanding. She occasionally required students to participate in small-group performance tasks to demonstrate a science principle. Scott believed the ultimate test of her own teaching was whether students could articulate in writing the principles she taught. She incorporated all types of writing into her curriculum, including reports, essays, and poetry.

Darlene Wood was a first-year teacher with certification in social studies and math. Her sixth-grade social studies class focused on world geography, the title of the available textbook. Wood, however, rarely used the book, concentrating instead on group

Team Members: Experience and Areas of Emphasis

Nina Scott—Science	**Darlene Wood—Social Studies**
• Experience: 4 years • Group/performance tasks • Open-note tests • Incorporates writing	• Experience: 1st year teacher • Individual/group projects • Learning contracts • Minimal use of textbook
David Campbell—Math	**Betsy Rogers—Language Arts**
• Experience: 10 years • Favors direct instruction • Some collaborative groups • Incorporates writing	• Experience: 17 years • Reading/writing portfolios • Reading/writing workshops • Direct instruction in skill areas

and individual projects and learning contracts. Prior to becoming a full-time teacher, she became familiar with the team system at Wakefield as a student teacher.

David Campbell, with ten years' experience, had an elementary 1–8 certification and a master's degree in special education. He enjoyed working with middle school students, often telling jokes and funny stories to get his point across in math. Despite his consistent belief in the value of direct, teacher-led instruction, Campbell changed his classroom style substantially over the past few years. Before Wakefield's implementation of the team concept, his students could be found seated in straight rows working diligently out of the textbook. With the implementation of teams, they sat at tables in collaborative groups and used many different types of materials to study and understand math concepts. Campbell also systematically incorporated writing into his daily lessons.

Rogers' language arts class emphasized developing fluency in reading and writing. In addition to conducting whole-group classroom instruction, she required students to produce extensive responses to independent reading assignments and to write for many different audiences and purposes. They created reading/writing portfolios as part of the assessment process. Rogers described her classroom as a reading/writing workshop supplemented by direct instruction in specific skill areas.

This sixth-grade team was well known for its emphasis on student-centered methods, but this prompted criticism from some colleagues. They contended that, because of the team's thematic and hands-on approach to teaching, students had a hard time adjusting to the instructional styles of more traditional teachers in later grades.

THE UNIT

The idea of writing and field-testing a student-generated unit began with a request for grant proposals. The principal of Wakefield Middle School asked Rogers if she would be interested in applying for a state grant to write a model instructional unit. Rogers' proposal outlined a student-centered approach to learning that could be implemented as a unit within the existing team framework at Wakefield. When the proposal was funded, Rogers formed a planning committee for the unit consisting of herself, the seventh-grade team leader, the eighth-grade team leader, the principal, and a university professor who worked in a collaborative relationship with the school. All agreed that this unit, implemented across the three grade-level teams, should be designed to include learning experiences that would be developmentally appropriate for the learners involved. After discussing current middle school concepts and developmental philosophy, the faculty decided to base the unit on student-centered curricula using the philosophy and research of James Beane.

The committee endorsed Beane's notion that units should begin by asking young adolescents how they see themselves, what questions they have about themselves, and what questions they have about the larger world. In this approach, students look for patterns within their questions, and themes emerge. With teacher guidance, students decide what to know in relation to the questions, how they want to find out, and how and with whom they want to share their results. In theory, this allows students to develop various learning styles and multiple intelligences in a context that recognizes different developmental levels, strengths, and abilities.

Planning committee members circulated a preliminary outline of instructional guidelines to participating teachers:

Instructional Guidelines

1. Tell students we will be using a new approach to learning. "In most of the past year, teachers have decided what you will learn, how you will learn it, and what you will do to demonstrate your learning. In the next three-week unit, you will have more to say about each of those three things." Explain the process (which follows).
2. Tell students we have decided to focus on the theme of "Transitions." (Write it on the board.) Ask them, "What do you think that word means?" They may want to speculate, some students may know, and others may want to look it up in various dictionaries. (*The American Heritage Student's Dictionary* defines "transition" as "the process or an example of changing or passing from one form, state, subject, or place to another.") See if, as a group, you can formulate a working definition, then ask students for examples of some transitions. This will allow you to see how well they understand the concept as well as provide concrete examples for others to consider.
3. Then tell students we have come up with an essential question that will help guide the overall learning of students at all grade levels. It is, "How have the transitions that children make from childhood to adulthood changed as the self, school, community, and the world have changed?" (Write this on the board also.) Ask students to think for one minute, then discuss with a partner near them, what they think that question means. Then invite them to share ideas about the meaning of the question (not possible answers to it) in the large group, calling on students randomly whether they have raised hands or not.
4. Tell them we will focus on transitions within a particular time period, with students at each grade level looking at a different time period. Sixth graders will look back at the transitions from childhood to adolescence, a more concrete activity in keeping with their developmental level. Seventh graders will look around at the transitions taking

place within adolescence. Eighth graders will look ahead at the changes and decisions taking place from adolescence to young adulthood, a more abstract challenge that is developmentally appropriate for these older students. (Write the time period for your grade level on the board.)

5. There are several ways to approach the next activity, which is helping the students relate to the Transitions theme and the essential question. We have listed them in the order most in keeping with Beane's approach to curriculum development, starting with a more open-ended approach. Recognizing that some groups of students may not know how to respond, we have provided three ways of approaching the same question, each providing more structure (see Exhibit D for details of these strategies). We ask kids to be risk-takers in their writing and thinking, and this would be a good opportunity to model that behavior for them.

6. Another way to help students see how the world has changed and how that might affect the transitions they make from childhood to adulthood is to have students interview adults about their transitions. Talking with parents might be an easy starting place, though students should have the option of interviewing anyone more than twenty years older than themselves in case they are not comfortable interviewing their parents. Invite students to choose questions from the ones discussed previously in which they are most interested. Their goal is to find out about the kinds of transitions adults faced and compare them with those of current middle school students. Students should write questions about the topics or areas of interest to them and the class, but also include some open-ended questions that allow the adult to mention transitions that current students may not face. For example, students might ask about options adults felt they had for careers and training after high school, if that topic is of interest to the students. An open-ended question about other concerns the adult had about life after high school might elicit comments about facing a military draft, a concern current students do not face. This is where you'll need to do a mini-lesson on interviewing, and you could make that lesson extensive as time will allow. At the least, students need to check their questions for biased wording, completeness, and whether they will elicit comments on topics which students can't anticipate. They might want to practice interviewing peers and taking notes while listening to get experience. Discuss how they will record answers and suggest that they might use a tape recorder, if one is available. That way they can go back afterward to add to the notes they took during the interview.

7. Discuss results of the interviews. What aspects of school, community, and nation/world have changed? (Record on board or overhead.) How did those changes seem to affect the transitions of the people you interviewed compared to your transitions? (Example: "My mom didn't have to worry about being pressured to take drugs 'cause no one in school did that kind of stuff when she was in middle school, so she had less to worry about. On the other hand, she talked about the Cold War and being afraid we were going to get nuked by the Russians, and that's not something I ever think about.") Through this discussion, develop the idea that students' personal lives and concerns are impacted by what is going on in the school, community, and nation/world.

8. Here's where we start to get convergent and decide which questions (among the many that have been discussed) students would like to investigate further. Get students into groups of about four using pre-existing groups, random assignment (number off, cards, birthdays, etc.), or your decision about groups that would provide diversity of opinion. Ask them to share the questions considered previously and see if the group can reach consensus on three to six questions they feel would be of interest to most group members. They can start with questions that appeared on

several students' individual lists or on the board through various class discussions, and can add others that arise as a result of their discussion in the group.
9. After the groups have had time to work, the teacher should then invite students to contribute questions to a class list, writing them on the overhead or blackboard. Collect the small group lists to be sure to have a hard copy of all ideas. Invite students to see which questions or areas of interest the class seems to have in common. Agree on a list of questions that are of interest to many (but not necessarily all or even a majority of) class members.
10. Then invite students to think about how they might go about answering these questions. This would be a good time to repeat the procedure of thinking/writing individually for five minutes, then discussing with small groups, then sharing in large groups. Encourage them to think beyond traditional sources like textbooks, encyclopedias, etc., since it is unlikely those sources will have the answers anyway. They might need suggestions about other ways to find out: interviews; look at documents or movies or news shows of the time period; call or write to agencies like substance abuse centers or police departments; design surveys; etc.
11. Students then need to think about a final product and audience. Only then will you know what content and/or skills need to be taught, unless as a team you have predetermined some outcomes that your students need before testing. In that case, teachers need to guide students in the direction in the following discussion. After the discussion about personal and global concerns regarding transitions, have students brainstorm ideas for a sixth, seventh, or eighth-grade product to explore and share their answers to the questions that have been chosen as well as a real world audience. Guide them to think about different products they could produce, including those involving drama, technology, music, publishing, art, etc.
12. Teachers should compare questions and ideas for products across groups of students within the team. You should then either take the most popular suggestions back to the students for discussion/consensus/vote or choose the questions and products that best meet the needs of students on the team.
13. Think about content and process skills in your discipline that would relate to students' questions and ways to answer their questions. Then think about general content/skills that would also be relevant and needed in order to carry out their investigation. Meet with your team to share lists and discuss possibilities. This might also be a good time to go through the list of learner academic expectations from the state to choose two or three on which to focus. What skills, abilities, and concepts can you teach in order that kids create products high in quality with respect to both content and communicating effectively with their chosen audience?

TEAM DECISIONS

The committee decided to approach planning this unit with two modifications of Beane's theory. First, instead of allowing individual themes to emerge, all three grade levels agreed to implement the same theme–Transitions. Second, the teachers presented students with the essential question "How have the transitions that children make from childhood to adulthood changed as they change and their schools, communities, and the world have changed?" rather than having students generate the question. The teachers believed this would provide some structure while still assigning students primary responsibility for the substance and format of the unit.

The format of the unit plan also followed the state Department of Education curriculum framework[1] including the following elements:

- Establishing organizers
- Addressing academic expectations
- Formulating essential questions
- Planning a culminating performance
- Facilitating the culminating performance

The planning committee discussed and predicted possible outcomes for the unit. Because of the student-centered nature of the unit, however, teachers would be responsible for little prior planning once the unit began. Though the experimental unit would not be graded, assessment would take place based largely on a student-generated rubric; teachers in turn would use this rubric in their assessment of each group's product as well as of individual contributions. The unit would last approximately three weeks.

UNIT SNAPSHOT

Initially, sixth-grade students generated a list of possible questions and suggested ways in which each might be developed within the unit. Through the teamwide questioning process guided by the teachers, the students determined that they were interested in finding out more about five topics: the transition to seventh grade in Wakefield Middle School, the transitions of twelve- and thirteen-year-olds throughout history, the transitions in society caused by medical and technological advances, environmental issues, and issues of crime and violence. Students were thinking on a more sophisticated and ambitious level than the planning committee had anticipated.

Led by their teachers, the sixth graders subsequently discussed what form their culminating performances might take. This discussion raised some practical concerns for Rogers. Two cheerleaders had suggested a float for the annual spring festival parade. According to their plan, the float would display facts about transitions in crime and violence, AIDS statistics, statistics on rain forest depletion and its consequences, and historical perspective on the transitions of twelve- and thirteen-year-olds. The two girls' enthusiasm was contagious, and the idea quickly spread throughout the sixth-grade team. More than a little concerned, the teachers were immediately worried about the appropriateness, logistics, and legality of the idea. After a lengthy discussion about appropriate audience, students gave up the float idea and instead chose to create a video magazine with segments done by different study groups on each of the above topics. This magazine would then be shared with other students in the school and district. Rogers' team breathed a collective sigh of relief.

---

[1]Adapted from Kentucky Department of Education. (1995). *Transformations: Kentucky's Curriculum Framework* (Vol. 2). Frankfort: Author.

Soon after, Rogers led the students in a brainstorming session to create an assessment rubric for the video magazine. Using a "Quality/Not Yet Quality" continuum, students identified properties of good and poor video productions (Exhibit B); Rogers kept a record of suggestions on an overhead projector. She made copies of the overhead for students to use as a guide for production and to use with the group evaluation tool at the end of the process (see Exhibits A–D). Though the team agreed that these categories could easily have been modified into an actual scoring rubric, the teachers agreed that grading would not yet be appropriate given the experimental nature of the unit.

For their contribution, Rogers' students decided, through intensive discussion, to create a video timeline of the major historical transitions that twelve- and thirteen-year-olds had faced in American history. The class had previously discussed what they knew about timelines and American history. A library visit yielded varied topics to script the skits for the video timeline: Michael and Jimmy were writing a rap for the introduction to each segment of the video time line; Nick, Tracy, and Adrienne practiced their slavery scene of the early 1800s; Maria and Cindy were painting a backdrop for their child labor scene of the early 1900s; and three other students continued to research the role of newly arriving immigrants. A small group of students worked on a school survey to complete their section on twelve- and thirteen-year-olds of the future.

When students asked questions, Rogers typically responded, "Did you consider all the possibilities? If so, this is your unit—you decide."

Rogers was impressed by how diligently and creatively the students approached their tasks without initial direct instruction. Michael, for example, was becoming quite a leader. It was his idea to introduce each segment of the time line with an historical rap, and he was keeping the other students on track. Other students were displaying considerable creativity and resourcefulness.

STUDENT REACTIONS

Rogers sat alone at a table in her classroom reflecting on the Transitions unit that had just been completed. The team teachers had asked students to write their thoughts in journals using the following questions:

1. What did you like about the unit?
2. What did you dislike about it?
3. Did anything about the unit make you feel proud?
4. What is something that you learned by doing the unit?

Now she was anxious to read the responses. She placed the plastic container filled with dog-eared spiral notebooks next to her on the floor, then randomly selected a small stack. She began to read.

> I liked how we got to choose the group we were in. I liked how we organized it all by ourselves. I like doing things with activities that I have to plan and work on. I have a better

idea of things if I invent it. I disagreed with some of the things my class did. One was the commercial. One group from my class did it all. They didn't ask for suggestions or if anybody else wanted to be in it. My group had one leader for endangered animals. When she wasn't there everything went wrong—No leaders. Nothing made me feel proud. I learned about the very few rain forests. Many endangered animals are becoming extinct. I also learned that we have more responsibilities ahead of us for 2000.

    I liked having the freedom to choose the activities and work that we did. Also, the teachers made it fun, which I think is important. The video magazine was a lot of fun, but I learned a lot from it too! I think this was one of the better units we've done because we know what we like and it helps when we're doing something we like to do. I didn't like the fact that some of the group members goofed off the whole time while others put a lot of effort into it. It's not really fair, especially since they're getting the same grade. Other than that everything was great! I was kind of proud of myself and my group because this was challenging but we pulled through at the last minute! I learned that AIDS has become a war worldwide, and that a cure is doubtful for the year 2000. The percentage of people who have developed AIDS has increased a lot and is going to keep rising if something isn't done, especially in ages 15–25.

    What I liked about the Transitions unit is we had a lot of control over what we did. I also liked doing the video because it helped us learn how much goes into just ten minutes of video. What I didn't like about the unit was we didn't have enough time for the video. What I'm proud of is our whole tape. I think all of the groups worked hard. I learned a lot about how much time and effort goes into a video. I also learned a lot about video cameras and editing and filming things.

    In the Transitions unit I liked that the kids got to decide how they wanted to work to do the video. It gave us a chance to use our creative minds, and we got the chance to show the teachers what we've learned. I disliked that some people didn't get into the groups they wanted. I had a good idea for the crime and violence group but it didn't get in. I liked the whole video because we made it. I learned that seventh grade is about the same as this year. The work is just a little harder and they have a little more to do.

    I liked filming ourselves. That way we know what we look like when other people are watching. I liked staying in one classroom most of the time. You get used to the teacher. I don't think we had enough time to film. Because there were so many groups we had to hurry and get it right the first time. I was proud that the students thought up a lot of the ideas. The teachers just pretty much motivated us. I learned a lot about filming and teamwork. I learned that a group has to work as a team to get anything done.

    I liked that we made most of the decisions. Everything wasn't picked out or planned. We didn't have enough time to make improvements. I'm proud that we made a video that many people will watch. We weren't just doing it for a grade. It counted for something.

BACK TO THE LOUNGE

After each teacher had the opportunity to read the students' comments, Rogers called a meeting to address the team's concerns. "You have all said that students for the most part have been more motivated and better behaved, that all sorts of leadership and other talents have emerged, and that if we weren't crunched by the grant deadline, the products would be very high quality. Kids have incorporated into the unit all kinds of concepts like ecosystems, renewable resources, historical timelines, statistics, the impact of technology on society, health issues, the impact of violence on society, the developmental stages of early adolescents, and self-concept. All indicators are that, for students, this has been collectively our most successful unit."

"True, but how can we be sure that we couldn't do this better in a format we're more at ease with?" Campbell countered. "I can't help wondering whether Beane is just one more guru of the month we're following just because he's popular with the National Middle School Association people."

Wood seemed torn. "We talked about Beane's model in my university classes, and at the time it sure seemed consistent with everything else I had learned about early adolescent development. But David has a point. How do we know it's better than what we would otherwise do? More than that—with all the teaching strategies I was exposed to in school, I wonder about being 'locked in' with this approach. Also, I hate to say it, but I have to worry about some more basic issues—my first year evaluations and the fact that this kind of thing doesn't fit clearly within my internship status guidelines."

"I have to agree," Scott offered, "it puts us all as teachers in an awkward position. Beyond this experiment, there remains a question of accountability with the whole concept. How could we explain a student's grade with this kind of curriculum, where students decide what to study and generate their own rubrics for assessment? What happens when students accustomed to this kind of work have classes with more conventional teachers? If I taught this way on a more regular basis, would my students learn enough science concepts so I could feel I did my job?"

"I understand your concerns about the unit," Rogers responded. "Your concern about accountability and content coverage has been less of a problem for me because language arts is so process oriented that I know kids can learn and use those skills studying most any content. But I have given some thought to this grade business also. Parents may see this as a waste of time, though we're clearly seeing high-quality learning taking place for many of the students. It is hard finding a match between this new approach to learning and the old system of accountability. And with the unpredictability of the questions on the statewide performance assessment tests, there's no guarantee our kids' learning will be reflected there, either." The others nodded in agreement.

"I'm not really sure what I think yet," Rogers continued slowly. "On one hand, we have to admit that this approach is working for our students as far as motivation and self-concept are concerned. Content is certainly being integrated, and students are learning processes they need to know. On the other hand, I hear your concerns. And," she turned to face Wood, "I certainly wouldn't want to do anything to discourage you from experimenting further or to make you uneasy about your status. I'm sure we all appreciate that there is a certain amount of risk taking inherent in attempting something like this, especially on a more sustained basis."

Rogers paused, for the moment unsure how to continue. From her own observations of the implementation of the unit on three teams at sixth, seventh, and eighth-grade levels, she knew many of the positive student outcomes that the planning committee had predicted were taking place: increased student motivation, decreased discipline problems, ownership of learning, and creativity.

While Rogers understood the team's concerns, she remained confident in the philosophy of student-centered curricula. Moreover, she had hoped that implementing more units like this one would help refine the process. With the team's misgivings, however, it was uncertain whether this would take place.

"We can't afford to ignore how successful this has been for the students," she said. "On the other hand, I have the highest respect for all of you, both personally and professionally, and your concerns need to be considered. I guess the question we all need to think about is how to begin implementing reforms like this in a way that works for students and teachers alike."

EPILOGUE

After several follow-up discussions in the spring, participating teachers decided to retain aspects of the student-centered curriculum that had proven successful and to continue with varying degrees of interdisciplinary coordination.

The beginning of the next academic year, however, coincided with long overdue structural renovations at Wakefield. The physical constraints on flexible learning and teaching strategies quickly became evident; the unpredictable pace of renovation meant that classes had to be frequently evacuated—usually to the cafeteria so that teachers could be heard over the din of construction. The plans for continuing innovation were soon set aside in favor of what Rogers called "survival mode"—highly structured, traditional teacher-led methods that seemed necessary in the face of the logistical chaos brought on by renovation. For Rogers there was one source of inspiration. Despite their earlier reservations, the teachers on her team expressed some regret over the delay in expanding on their earlier successes. Rogers was particularly intrigued by Wood's newfound confidence in student-centered curriculum and her vocal concerns about "lost momentum."

For her own part, Rogers knew that if a student-centered approach was to reemerge successfully, it would have to come from other team members. "I must adopt a wait-and-see approach and put my own enthusiasm for moving ahead on the back burner."

REFERENCES AND SELECTED BIBLIOGRAPHY

Apple, M. W., & Beane, J. A. (Eds.). (1995). *Democratic schools*. Alexandria, VA: Association for Supervision and Curriculum Development.

Atwell, N. (1987). *On the middle: Working, reading and learning with adolescents*. New York: Boynton/Cook.

Beane, J. (1990). *Middle school curriculum: From rhetoric to reality*. Columbus, OH: National Middle School Association.

Brophy, J., & Alleman J. (1991). Activities as instructional tools: A framework for analysis and evaluation. *Educational Researcher*, 20(4), 9–23.

Cook, N. (1994). Mario is missing. *Technology & Learning*, 14(4), 7–13.

George, P., Stevenson, C., Thomason, J., & Beane, J. (1992). *The middle school and beyond*. Alexandria, VA: Association for Supervision and Curriculum Development.

Lipsitz, J. (1984). *Successful schools for young adolescents.* Brunswick, NJ: Transaction.
McDonough, L. (1991). Middle level curriculum: The search for self and social meaning. *Middle School Journal,* 23(2), 29–35.
Shubert, W. H. (1994). Toward lives worth sharing: A basis for integrated curriculum. *Educational Horizons,* 73(1), 25–30.
Spady, W. G. (1994). Choosing outcomes of significance. *Educational Leadership,* 51(6), 18–22.
Vars, G. F. (1991). Integrated curriculum in historical perspective. *Educational Leadership,* 49(2), 14–15.

EXHIBIT A

Questions Raised by Students Planning the "Transitions" Unit

The team worked through the question-generating process around the first question (What do we want to know?) and came up with these types of questions:

When and how will I die?
Will there be a cure for AIDS?
Will my kids be exposed to the same violence and crime I am as a sixth grader?
How will technology in the future affect me?
Will there be any land left with the growth in the community?
Will there be any trees left?
Will the ozone layer hold?
Will potential racial/ethnic wars affect me as I get older?
Will (or how will) I be able to handle peer pressure?
Why are there guns in school?
Why do middle school and high school kids smoke, drink, and take drugs?
What will seventh grade be like?
Who will be my future partner? And how will we live?
How will the school renovation affect me?

They synthesized the large list into seven team questions:

1. What will be important in the transition to seventh grade?
2. What impact will violence and crime have on my life?
3. How will diseases and medical advances affect me?
4. How will I use technology in the future?
5. What environmental issues will be important?
6. How will population growth affect my future?
7. How will transitions in governments affect my society?

The team decided that all these questions could fit under the guiding question "What does the future hold for our class?" Students rank-ordered their choice of questions for work groups, and the last two questions were dropped owing to little interest. However, the first question regarding transitions to seventh grade had enough interest for two subgroups.

EXHIBIT B

Student-Generated Quality Continuum for Video Productions

Quality	**Not Yet Quality**
• informative	• not informative
• accurate	• inaccurate
• organized	• unorganized
• no deviations from the topic	• gets off topic
• entertaining	• boring
• creative	• not original
• has an audience	• targets wrong people
• clarity of content (vocabulary)	• jumbled
• time limit (appropriate length)	• too short/long
• interconnections of groups	• no communication
• good camera work	• audience cannot understand video
• appearance (lends credibility)	• actors/interviewers not dressed appropriately
• nonoffensive	• racist/sexist/bad language

EXHIBIT C

Description of Culminating Project for the "Transitions" Unit Video Magazine

Participating students brainstormed about a potential audience for the questions they were exploring. They decided that their audience would be other middle school students. They then brainstormed the format that would be needed to share their information. The students on the team made a list of suggestions, then made a decision to create a team video magazine, which would have different segments to share their findings. This video magazine would be shared with the rest of the school through the school's closed-circuit TV system, and they would also send copies of the videotape to the other middle schools in the county.

Each student chose the question that he or she was most interested in exploring, and those with the same choice formed a separate small work team to investigate the answers to their particular question and plan their own segment of the video magazine. The question about seventh-grade transitions had enough interest for two class work teams. Segments on the video magazine included the following:

1. Introduction
2. Transitions of twelve- and thirteen year-olds throughout U.S. history
3. Transitions to seventh grade at Wakefield Middle School
4. Transitions in medical predictions and possible advances in the next ten years
5. Transitions and possibilities in technology in the next ten years
6. Transitions in violence and crime in America and its impact on kids
7. Transitions in the environment and its impact on kids
8. Closure

One student on the team acted as "host" of the video magazine to introduce segments and provide some narration between segments. Each segment was planned, written, and filmed by the students involved in their own particular interest group.

The segment on the transitions of twelve- and thirteen-year-olds throughout American history was presented as a video time line in which different eras of American history were researched and portrayed through the eyes of preadolescents of the time. The next segment on the transition to seventh grade in this particular school was handled through interviews and varied types of real-life reporting from the site. The grim statistics of teens with AIDS and its impact on society were revealed in a student-written and -performed skit in the segment on the transitions in medicine. A student news broadcast, complete with commercials, reported the advancement of technology and its effect on the lives of today's students. The segments of the magazine dealing with environmental issues included several activities about pollution, recycling, and the depletion of the rain forest and what preadolescents can do to help.

The rubric, developed by student discussion, about what would be quality and what would not be quality for the video magazine, was used to assess the final product.

EXHIBIT D

Strategies for Students to Personally Relate to Theme and Essential Question

Strategy I

Ask students to think about questions they personally have related to the overall theme and essential question. You might start with, "What kinds of questions do you have about changes in yourself from (time period)?" If students seem unclear about the question, you might want to volunteer some of your experiences at the time period under consideration, e.g., "When I was in junior high, none of my friends even thought about using drugs or drinking, though I suspect some kids (not my friends) did smoke cigarettes. I wondered why some kids did smoke, though." Give students about five minutes to think and write down several questions in which they are genuinely interested.

After this, give them another five minutes to think about questions they have on a more global scale. "What are some questions you have about changes in the world or country or our community and how that might affect you?" A personal example might be "I lived in Miami at the time when lots of refugees were coming over from Cuba. I wondered how that might affect my life, if I would have to learn Spanish, how they would fit into our school and city."

Strategy II

If your students seem to be in need of more structure, you might create these scenarios for them to consider:

Sixth Grade. "Think back to when you were in fourth and fifth grade. Remember what you looked like, what you liked to do after school, what you did in school, what was going on in the world, etc. Jot down a few ideas you have." Give students three to four minutes to record ideas, circulating to ensure that all are participating. Invite them to share ideas in a class discussion. Now ask them to think about what they would have wanted to know about themselves as sixth graders. "If you had had a middle school student come visit with you in fourth grade, what questions would you have had for this guest about the changes that would take place in you and your world over the two years from fourth to sixth grade?"

Seventh Grade. "Think about the changes you are going through right now in middle school. It might help to think back to how you've changed just in the year and a half that you have been here. Think about some eighth graders you know and how you might change even more between now and the end of eighth grade. Take four or five minutes to write some questions you have about the changes you and your peers are going through during your three years in middle school, then we'll share ideas and see if we can come up with questions of interest to you."

Eighth Grade. "Think about the questions you have about the changes that will affect you over the next three to five years. Imagine that a high school senior or college sophomore, perhaps *you* several years in the future, can travel back in time to answer all of your questions. What would you want to know about how you will change? What about how your school will change? Your town? The country and world?"

Strategy III

List four categories on the board: self, school, community, nation/world. Ask students to think about changes they have experienced or can imagine within each category, jotting down ideas on a piece of paper. For example, the category of self might include physical changes in the body, dating, concrete to abstract thinking, what's fun to do recreationally, privileges and responsibilities at home, etc. You could also pass out copies of the newspaper (world/nation and local sections) and ask students to look for world, national, or community issues. Take about five minutes for this, and circulate to be sure all students are recording ideas. Then, first as a small group, then a large one, or as a whole class, ask students to share their ideas as the group brainstorms possible areas of change within each category. Using this list of topics as a starting point, ask students to think about at least three questions related to transitions that she/he is personally interested in investigating. Keep in mind the time period on which your grade level is focusing. Personal examples might include sixth grade, "Who will my friends be in middle school and how will I choose them?"; seventh grade, "What kind of decisions might I have to make in middle school about using alcohol, tobacco, or drugs?"; eighth grade, "What kind of career do I want to be involved in as an adult?"

To help students see how the topics listed under school, community, and nation/world might affect them, ask them to think about ones that might have changed from previous years. (Student example: "I saw an article about gangs and wonder if kids today are more concerned about violence than they used to be three years ago.") Also, invite them to consider which world, national, or community changes might affect their own transitions. For example, changes in technology might affect the kind of education they get.

DISCUSSION QUESTIONS

1. Describe the situation from each of the following perspectives: the teachers on the sixth-grade team, Rogers, the students, the parents.
2. The planning team for this unit felt that a student-generated approach would help meet their goal of using a variety of instructional strategies to encourage the development of critical thinking and performance skills. How well does Beane's approach, as implemented here, appear to meet the intent of this principle? What are the costs and benefits of such an approach? Among other considerations, include the following:
    - Scott's concerns with the thematic curricula center on her awareness of standard expectations for content coverage. What are the implications of having either students or teachers choose topic areas that do not converge with conventional content coverage of particular disciplines?
    - Some educational reformers assert that "less is more" in terms of content coverage. How do you interpret this view, and so you agree or disagree?
    - Do some subjects lend themselves to a thematic approach (e.g., Rogers states that language arts is process oriented anyway), whereas others need to be more tightly sequenced? Would your discipline lend itself to thematic teaching? Why or why not?
3. How important is a match between a teacher's natural teaching style and the format of instruction for successful learning to take place? Take into account the following:
    - Wood prefers much more structure and preplanning. To what degree should she sacrifice her teaching philosophy for team goals?
    - In the past, Campbell has effectively presented information and skills in a teacher-centered way, and he insists that at least some of his students seem to prefer his usual style. Should he change his teaching style if it has been effective for students? How can he be certain which style is the most effective way of teaching?
    - Are there ways teachers could modify the unit to meet their individual teaching styles and goals? Would these compromise the strengths of the unit and undermine its effectiveness?
4. Consider the advantages and disadvantages of cooperative learning as described in the case.
    - The state reform initiatives support a greater use of group work. Scott has noticed several students who do not seem to be contributing to the group projects on a consistent basis. In what ways might she ensure that all students participate equally?
    - Scott and the others also know that just working on a project does not mean that students understand the concepts being studied. In a method that uses group projects to demonstrate learning of concepts and skills, how can teachers distinguish and assess how much each individual has learned?
5. Consider the issue of assessment.

- Scott wonders how to explain a student's report card grade to parents when she has only a few grades in her grade book. How should the team communicate to parents what students have learned and how they have shown their learning? Are there intermediate assessments that could be used to provide a yardstick of learning to both parents and students? What would you suggest?
- Rogers and Scott raise the question of accountability, particularly in light of statewide assessment tests. Despite an increased emphasis on writing, the new tests remain very much discipline based. Scott and Wood wonder how well students will perform when their learning has been through interdisciplinary, thematic units. What are some options for handling this and the costs and benefits of each?
- Assess Rogers' guiding questions for the students' journals. What additional information would you like to have and how would you go about getting it? How would you use the information?
- The end-of-unit student evaluations as well as teachers' observations provide data for determining the effectiveness of the unit. Based on this information, explain whether you agree or disagree with Rogers's claim of student success.

6. The members of the teaching team feel the burden of their collective reputation as the innovators in the school. They believe that some teachers are waiting for them to give up. In contrast, other teachers may be interested in trying out similar units if the team is successful. How might these pressures affect the team's reaction to the unit?
   - What do you see as the advantages/disadvantages for a beginning teacher to be part of a teaching team? How would you feel about being part of this experimental program?
   - Some colleagues believe that students have a hard time adjusting to the more traditional approach of teachers in subsequent grades. If you were a teacher attempting reform, how would you explain this to parents who express concern that their children may not be prepared in later grades?

7. Campbell wonders aloud whether Beane's approach is truly effective or whether his method is simply another fashionable approach embraced by theorists.
   - How would you suggest that teachers assess new ideas that they have not seen implemented? What should be the basis for teachers' decisions to embark on voluntary innovations? List specific criteria.
   - Each of the team members is at a different level of experience. How might this affect their responses to change?

8. Review questions 1 through 7 in Exhibit A.
   - Which questions were addressed by students in the unit? How likely is it that students will develop an in-depth understanding of all the concepts in a three-week period? Consider whether this unit sacrificed breadth and depth of content to student motivation and interest. As a teacher, how would you prioritize the most important concepts?
   - Are cognitive and affective goals mutually exclusive?

Case 6

9. Assume you are part of the interdisciplinary team for the third year. The renovations are completed, and the group has decided to try the interdisciplinary approach again, *but* with major refinements.
    - What refinements would you suggest and why? If there are elements of the unit that should be kept, identify which ones and explain why.

CASE 6

Discussion Question	Corresponding INTASC Principle
2	1 The teacher understands the concepts, tools of inquiry, and structures of the discipline(s) he or she teaches and can create learning experiences that make these aspects of subject matter meaningful for students.
5	8 The teacher understands and uses formal and informal assessment strategies to evaluate and ensure the continuous intellectual, social, and physical development of the learner.
6	10 The teacher fosters relationships with school colleagues, parents, and agencies in the larger community to support learning and well-being.
7	9 The teacher is a reflective practitioner who continually evaluates the effects of his/her choices and actions on others (students, parents, and other professionals in the learning community) and who actively seeks out opportunities to grow professionally.
8	5 The teacher uses an understanding of individual and group motivation and behavior to create a learning environment that encourages positive social interaction, active engagement in learning, and self-motivation.
	7 The teacher plans instruction based upon knowledge of subject matter, students, the community, and curriculum goals.

CASE SEVEN

Compromise and Defeat: A Power Struggle at Watermill

Will Watermill Middle School see major changes in class scheduling for its three grades? These changes hinge on the actions of a twelve-member school council scheduled to meet today at 4 P.M., one month before the summer recess. The pending vote may conclude a lengthy debate on the changes.

The School-Based Decision Making (SBDM) Council has been struggling for months to reach a decision by "consensus" according to its own bylaws. However, some observers think true consensus may be one of the casualties in a battle of opinions arising from three specific camps: a determined administrator, dedicated teachers, and concerned parents.

Contemplating today's 4 P.M. meeting, Jane Brinkman, middle school teacher and council member, wonders whether the working parents on the council will be able to attend, given the short notice of the meeting. She also thinks the last-minute notice may heighten the parents' level of mistrust of the principal, Jack Carnes.

THE CONFLICT

This debate on the future of the middle school all began when a last-minute agenda item surfaced at a regularly scheduled council meeting in February. Principal Carnes added a proposal to change the existing class design to an interdisciplinary, heterogeneous, nongraded middle school structure.

This new approach would ignore student age as the criterion for class assignments. Students would be grouped and regrouped based on their developmental level for various subjects within a teaching team. In effect, they would be with the same group of teachers for three years with some of the students (the eighth graders) leaving and new ones (sixth graders) entering each year.

A number of parents, both council members and nonmembers, were quite concerned that Carnes did not provide adequate support for his proposal. Where was the research to support this new approach to middle school structure? Carnes adamantly argued it was the core strategy necessary to achieve higher student performance, but he mentioned only briefly research that linked this approach to higher student achievement. The only documentation he provided was a one-sheet handout with eight points about how positive it was to mix the grade levels.

Parent complaints revealed they perceived Carnes' action as arrogant. "It might be related to his reputation as an expert, and the fact he has been invited to speak elsewhere on reform matters," a teacher attempted to explain.

Parents were generally opposed to the nongraded concept from the beginning and expressed fears about mixing sixth graders with eighth graders. They were worried that the younger students might face intimidation from the older ones. They were also concerned that Carnes' plan represented a dramatic change from the existing class schedule and structure at Watermill.

Although teacher reactions to Carnes' idea were mixed, many were seized by his enthusiasm and immediately threw their support behind the proposal. Jane Brinkman, a middle school math teacher with a widespread reputation as an excellent instructor, was one of the dissenters. She could see some advantages to the team idea but feared students would miss out by not being exposed to all of the teachers in the school during their three years at Watermill.

"Carnes' proposal for a continuing team concept was supposed to be a very positive thing, to build relationships between teachers and children—more like a family atmosphere," Brinkman said. "But from personal experience that goes back many years, I also see a lot of negatives with this concept. There are many teachers who don't work well with certain kids. And there are many kids who like certain adults. They wouldn't have a chance to experience other teachers. Plus, there are some very effective teachers in our eighth grade to whom these children would never be exposed. In addition, a teacher who specifically likes seventh-grade material would now have to change gears and prepare for grades six and eight."

THE SCHOOL AND THE SBDM COUNCIL

Watermill Middle School first opened its doors to sixth, seventh, and eighth graders in the late 1980s. Initially, the middle school concept, a clear departure from the traditional elementary and junior high school approaches, received negative community reaction. Frequent discipline problems drew unfavorable press coverage. The original principal was encouraged to leave when teachers developed mistrust, prompting them to request expansion of the SBDM Council from six to twelve members. Because Carnes had been a successful high school principal in the same district, with a reputation as a strict disciplinarian, he was selected for the Watermill position. The district gave him a mandate to improve all aspects of education at the school.

Carnes attacked the challenge with zeal and enthusiasm, holding tight to the belief that the students had been given a "bad rap." He believed his middle-school youngsters were capable of reaching high levels of excellence in every subject area. In his opinion, high student achievement was accomplished through proper discipline and a faculty deeply devoted to students.

When Carnes came on board, the SBDM Council had been functioning for one year. During his first year, the faculty voted to expand the council to twelve members—twice the membership recommended by state law. The council consisted of six teacher representatives, elected by faculty colleagues; four parents, elected by the parent organization; the principal; and another administrator. All parents on the council received extensive training.

Following established hiring procedures that were under the jurisdiction of the council, Carnes conducted searches to fill several teaching vacancies in the wake of recent retirements. The process proved contentious when some council members complained that Carnes had intentionally limited the list of viable candidates he presented to them.

"It was a not-so-neat experience, putting in all those hours, and then he picks who he wants," complained one of the teacher representatives. "But, on the other hand, principals have to make tough decisions that others may not understand. It's one of those plus-minus kind of things."

Others were not as sanguine about the results of the selection process.

"We really didn't have much of a choice and were forced to choose the candidates he wanted despite our supposed power," fumed a parent representative.

These complaints about the process had little impact; positions were eventually filled by new faculty members who apparently met Carnes' criteria for continuing his crusade for school reform.

Well before his proposed new structure, the principal applied for a state grant and received sufficient funding to move Watermill toward major instructional changes. "Education reform" became the buzzword throughout the school. Frequent meetings became an integral part of the school routine. Faculty spent time developing what for them were new teaching methods and participating in long-term planning sessions. Paperwork increased significantly for all faculty members. Meanwhile, student scores climbed while discipline problems showed a marked decrease.

THE PRINCIPAL

Jack Carnes came to the school district from out of state with what many considered a preconceived agenda for change. His twenty years in education included thirteen years of experience in the classroom and seven more as an administrator.

Not only did he arrive with high expectations for Watermill students, but he also held lofty goals for teachers. He continually declared that the best teachers "cared about kids." His operational definition of "caring" included spending considerable time and effort attending instructional planning meetings, teaching classes, and assessing students' work—without complaining, and sometimes without extra pay. Carnes felt this extra effort on everyone's part was the key to improving student performance.

The new principal set a demanding pace to implement reform. Within three years of his arrival at Watermill, his successes securing higher student achievement and good publicity for the school gave rise to his reputation as an expert in education reform.

Other principals frequently requested that he speak at state and local conferences. Carnes accepted all invitations, indicating he enjoyed his growing acclaim as a highly effective change agent.

THE PARENT

Holly Smith was flattered by her election as one of four parent representatives on the SBDM Council. She had three children, with her oldest just starting the sixth grade at Watermill. Although she had been extremely active as a tutor/volunteer at the elementary school, Watermill's previous history of discipline problems made her apprehensive about her new role as a council member. However, the chance to work with a new principal gave her hope, and she felt her role on the SBDM Council was to ensure a sound educational experience at the school for her children.

"I decided this was a good way to keep up with what was going on at school since my kids were entering that critical stage that determines the path they will walk in life," Smith said about the challenge of her new council position. "I was not currently working at a job and decided that my time could best be spent as a member of the SBDM Council. I was honored to be given the opportunity to affect my own children's education as well as the education of other students at Watermill."

THE TEACHER

Jane Brinkman had been teaching in the district for more than a decade and was well respected by students, teachers, and parents. Her selection as a teacher representative to the council was considered by most to be a well-deserved honor, reflected by her three successful reelection bids.

Brinkman expressed reservations about the new size and structure of the SBDM Council. Her primary concern was the amount of time needed for twelve people to exchange views and develop a sense of competence and fairness in making collective decisions.

"We need to remember that the council is something new," she said. "We are not used to being in positions of making even the smallest decision. We are used to having them made for us."

Because of its large membership, the council created a policy restricting open discussion at its meetings. Guests were allowed to speak at the beginning of meetings, but subsequent discussion was limited to council members, who could address only predetermined agenda items.

THE COMPROMISE

Time passed and the tension about restructuring classes at Watermill grew. It continued through two more council meetings with heated debate, but without resolution.

As the year drew on, Carnes was convinced the battle lines had been decided. The longer the discussion continued, the more confrontational the situation became. At the fourth council meeting to discuss the new middle-school proposal, Carnes lost patience and announced what he termed a "compromise."

"OK, this is it. I'm willing to place only the seventh and eighth graders in the non-graded structure, but that's as far as I'm willing to compromise," he said. "In fact, if you don't accept this compromise, then I'll tell you what I'm going to do with the sixth graders. I'll totally self-contain them, just like they were in elementary school again with no departmental subject matter and no changing classes or regrouping with other sixth graders. They will have the same teacher and classmates all day long, every day."

Jane Brinkman felt her stomach tighten in response to the principal's declaration. She folded her hands in her lap and thought, "This was what comes from having twelve people trying to reach a consensus." She was extremely aware of the fact many parents felt their voices were falling on deaf ears, even at SBDM Council meetings.

On the other hand, her fellow teachers on the council had been urging Brinkman to give Carnes' plan her vote of support. For the past two months, they had said, "All consensus means is that you think you can live with this idea. You don't have to be entirely for or against it, but if you can live with the decision, go along." Most teachers at Watermill favored the proposal.

By contrast, the parent representative, Holly Smith, couldn't believe her ears as she listened to Carnes. His solution was an ultimatum; why was he calling it a compromise?

"Fine," she stated emphatically. "Let the minutes show that I am only agreeing to this because I feel under threat that if I don't, kids will suffer from being in self-contained classrooms."

Despite her agreement, Smith remained confused. "I don't know what to do," she told herself. "After all, I have to work with this principal and these teachers over the next four years with my other children."

In a hushed conversation following Carnes' compromise announcement, Smith whispered to a community observer, "We couldn't find any parents who were really ready to accept that proposal. There were many parents who had begun coming to the meetings to express their opposition. They thought the older kids would negatively influence or intimidate the sixth graders.

"But this point of view didn't get heard," Smith continued. "When additional people were at the meetings, Mr. Carnes got nervous. He couldn't control the numbers. He doesn't like feeling out of control."

She continued to quietly share her concerns with the interested observer.

"When the proposal first came up, I said no to this idea," she whispered. "At that time, a split occurred between the parents and teachers. Originally, the teachers had mostly sided with us, then suddenly they were going against the parents. Immediately, we felt uneasy around them. We have been taking this stand by ourselves, except for Mrs. Brinkman, who agreed with us."

Smith glanced around the meeting room and continued. "When we left meetings, Mrs. Brinkman would talk to us and agree with us. But once she would see another teacher or Mr. Carnes coming, she would say, 'Oh, I have got to go! I can't be seen talking to you!' I don't think she realized how that made us parents feel."

Jane Brinkman acknowledged the support she and another teacher representative felt for the parents' point of view. She said she was reluctant to restrict students to one set of teachers, but the other teachers on the council kept urging her to just give Carnes' approach a try.

"You know, as tough as this is, I try hard to be tactful when I disagree," Brinkman said. "But I don't hesitate to do it."

She also offered some insight into the relationship between parent representatives on the SBDM Council and Carnes.

"I think parents thought the principal was intimidating, but I think parents generally feel this way about any principal," Brinkman said. "This is especially true of parents who are women, which all our parent council members are. They seemed to feel Mr. Carnes didn't think they knew what they were talking about or that their opinions were valid."

Brinkman continued with her assessment of the tension between the principal and the parents.

"He really does respect what they think," she said. "He has to look at them differently than he looks at educators because we come from different backgrounds. We all have one thing in common, and that's the kids. I am sure he respects the parents, but they just don't believe that. One parent told me she always felt like one of the male teachers talked down to her. I can see where parents might be a little intimidated. They have to work with all these people who are supposed to be 'authorities,' whatever that means."

Despite the requirement for consensus in the council's by-laws, Carnes felt the need for immediate action when he demanded passage of the "compromise" at the previous meeting. Carnes' compromise and the apparent administrative approval of it stunned parents and teachers alike. Jane Brinkman and Holly Smith each had to rethink her position. Smith felt certain the "compromise" proposal involved a behind-the-scenes arrangement between Carnes and the superintendent but had no evidence to support her conjecture. The superintendent had remained silent even though he was well aware of the parents' concerns about both the proposal and the questionable process by which it was introduced as a last-minute agenda item in violation of council by-laws. Smith was convinced this implied the superintendent's blessing.

THE VOTE

The only potential obstacle to Carnes' compromise could be today's council vote. As the sweeping hands of the clock on the wall of the council meeting room approached 4 P.M., Carnes reflected on the calls he had received from nearly all parent representatives protesting the time of the meeting. He recalled his conversation with the superintendent who had suggested rescheduling the meeting, but Carnes had refused to change the timing of his announcement of moving ahead with the new structure. He had received the council's reluctant go-ahead at the last meeting, and implementation of the compromise plan needed to begin immediately before more objections could be raised. He must have this final vote.

The four parent representatives on the council filtered into the meeting room along with the superintendent. Carnes took the floor quickly, explaining that the new structure would mix only seventh and eighth grades, and next year's seventh graders would remain with the same team for two years. There were no new surprises.

Both Brinkman and Smith were among the council members who voted for the principal's compromise. Brinkman decided there was little harm in experimenting with the new grouping arrangement. She felt it could be reevaluated and changed if it failed to succeed. Smith felt compelled to go along with the idea because she feared her children might suffer repercussions from Carnes if she voted against him.

Carnes' compromise passed.

EPILOGUE

Ironically, the principal saw the results of his plan for only the first year of implementation. Before the second year began, Carnes accepted a prestigious state education position to design and present workshops on educational leadership. His assistant principal, Mike Gohran, became acting principal responsible for the nongraded schedule. Within one year and concurrent with his full-time appointment to the principalship, Gohran pushed for the elimination of the nongraded plan, which had kept seventh graders on the same team for two years. The council approved the recommendation. Watermill returned to the old, pre-Carnes structure.

"I believe the teachers who had the seventh graders two years in a row did not want to have that happen again," Gohran explained. "They had a very challenging group of students."

A Parent's Reflection

Holly Smith felt locked in a no-win situation when the scheduling plan was pushed by Carnes. She was convinced that Carnes' compromise proposal could result in kids getting stuck with a "bad" teacher for their last two years at the middle school. She wished the principal and teachers favoring the change had produced research that demonstrated this scheduling approach would help improve student learning. However, she had failed to do any homework of her own involving research. Could she have found documented research to support her reservations?

Moreover, Smith was uncomfortable with the notion that Watermill had to be "first" to make changes. Why did Watermill have to lead education reform? The principal and teachers on the council assumed what they were doing was in the best interests of the children. She felt they dismissed any insights or expertise parents had to offer about their children. As a parent, Smith was convinced she also knew what was good for kids despite the seeming indifference toward her suggestions.

Smith's volunteer efforts at school all but disappeared the next year. Carnes' "controlling disposition" turned her away from volunteer activities at Watermill. She wasn't alone. All four parent representatives who had served during the compromise debate would not seek another term.

Privately, these parents said they did not want to waste their time in meetings in which they felt their views were not respected, but publicly they remained low-key about their reasons for not running again. All confided that they were worried about making their viewpoints too visible and their children vulnerable.

Smith was the last parent representative to reach the decision to leave the council. She said she didn't want to let Carnes "kick her out." In defiance, she completed her term just to prove she would not be "bullied." In all other school functions, she deliberately kept a low profile because she said she needed to "protect" her children.

Teacher Perspective

Jane Brinkman remained optimistic about the entire experience. She said she believed this series of sometimes painful events was necessary for the council, as a whole, to define the term *consensus*. To her, *consensus* meant reaching an agreement to "try it out for a while."

Brinkman knew the question of the two-year program for seventh and eighth graders remained unresolved, even though Carnes' compromise was accepted. She suspected that although the program became accepted, it would be questioned again by the faculty in the future and she was proven correct.

"That's the beauty of the SBDM Council," she explained. "The decisions we make are not written in stone. We can always take another look at the situation and change our minds."

Following the restructuring incident, the Watermill teachers voted almost unanimously to downsize the council back to six members. The return to a smaller council reinforced Brinkman's belief that achieving consensus was less difficult with fewer members.

She admitted, however, that parents were still limited in the expression of opinions in council meetings. She favored changing the restricted time policy to allow parents the freedom to discuss issues of interest whenever they surfaced at council meetings. But strong parental support for this change in policy never materialized.

One major change, in addition to the size of the council, took place. Approval of policy changes no longer required a complete consensus. Former parent member Holly Smith explained the change this way: "The by-laws have been changed with regard to policies. The council does not require complete consensus. They can do a majority vote. However, they need at least one parent to vote yes to change or make a new policy."

As a parent with children still in school, Brinkman knew that Smith was keeping tabs on council actions and said she felt comfortable with this new policy. But Smith's feelings about Carnes were reinforced by his departure to take a prominent state job.

"Mr. Carnes just wanted to stand out and be on the cutting edge," she said.

REFERENCES AND SELECTED BIBLIOGRAPHY

Berger, E. H. (1995). *Parents as partners in education* (5th ed.). Upper Saddle River, NJ: Merrill/Prentice Hall.

Canady, R. L., & Rettig, M. D. (1995). *Block scheduling: A catalyst for change in high schools.* Princeton, NJ: Eye on Education.

Conway, J. A., & Calzi, F. (1996). The dark side of shared decision making. *Educational Leadership, 53*(4), 45–49.

Educational Leadership (1995, November). Productive use of time and space. 53(3), 3–46 (entire issue)

Fullan, M. (1993). *Change forces: Probing the depths of educational reform.* London: Falmer.

Lindle, J. C. (1994). *Surviving school micropolitics: Strategies for administrators.* Lancaster, PA: Techtronics.

National Education Commission on Time and Learning. (1994). *Prisoners of time: Report of the National Education Commission on Time and Learning.* Washington, DC: U.S. Government Printing Office.

Schneider, B., & Coleman, J. S. (1993). *Parents, their children and schools.* Boulder, CO: Westview.

Sizer, T. R. (1986). Rebuilding: First steps by the coalition of essential schools. *Phi Delta Kappan, 68,* 38–42.

Sizer, T. R. (1990). *Horace's school: Redesigning the American high school.* Boston: Houghton Mifflin.

Steinberg, L.(1996). *Beyond the classroom: Why education reform efforts have failed.* New York: Simon & Schuster.

DISCUSSION QUESTIONS

1. How did this situation develop? What are some underlying issues in this case?
2. What is consensus?
   - Define the terms *consensus*, *compromise*, and *majority rule*.
   - How did each of the following people view consensus: Mr. Carnes? Jane Brinkman? Holly Smith?
3. Evaluate Carnes' leadership style.
   - What qualities seem to make him effective?
   - What qualities seem to cause problems?
   - Discuss other courses of action Carnes might have taken.
4. Consider the effects of the following factors on communication: council size, proportion of teacher to parent representatives, and degree of communication of representatives with their constituencies.
   - What processes might be set up to improve communication in this case?
   - What are the teachers' responsibilities regarding communication in the situation depicted in the case?
5. If micropolitics are the daily acts of influence, negotiation, and participation in the way things get done in school, what is micropolitical about this case?
   - What power issues are there? How much power does the council really have?

- How are claims for legitimacy made and supported?
- What apparent exchanges or bargains are made?
6. If you had been a teacher representative on the council, what would you have done? Explain your position.
7. In discussing the role of parents on the council, Jane Brinkman states that Carnes "has to look at them [parents] differently than he looks at educators."
    - Identify what parents can bring to school governance.
    - Identify what teachers can bring.
    - Should parents have a significant role in school governance? Why or why not?
    - Do you agree with Brinkman's position on parental involvement? Elaborate on your response.
    - What, if anything, did the school lose when those parents (and possibly others) "gave up?"
8. INTASC Principal 5 calls for the teacher to use "an understanding of individual and group motivation and behavior to create a learning environment that encourages positive social interaction, active engagement in learning, and social motivation." How might nongraded grouping affect a teacher's achievement of this principle?
    - What are possible negative effects? Evaluate, for example, the parents' concern that older students would negatively influence or intimidate sixth graders.
    - What are possible positive effects? Consider, for example, a student's opportunity to progress according to her interests and abilities rather than her chronological age.
9. Consider Jane Brinkman's role in this experience.
    - What else might she have done to influence the results before the compromise was reached?
    - Once a compromise was reached, would it have been appropriate for her to reach out to the parents to help them find some "good" in the new structure? Why or why not?
    - If so, how might she have reached out to the parents?
10. Do you agree with Brinkman's definition that *consensus* means to agree to "try something for awhile?"
    - Is this a workable definition? Why or why not?
    - Once institutional change is effected, how easy is it to change again?
    - How long should an educational reform be tried out before it can be fairly assessed? What are some factors to consider?
    - Do you think Carnes' departure from the school impacted the life of this reform attempt? How and why?

CASE 7

Discussion Question	Corresponding INTASC Principle
4	6 The teacher uses knowledge of effective verbal, nonverbal, and media communication techniques to foster active inquiry, collaboration, and supportive instruction in the classroom.
5, 7, 9	10 The teacher fosters relationships with school colleagues, parents, and agencies in the larger community to support learning and well being.
8	5 The teacher uses an understanding of individual and group motivation and behavior to create a learning environment that encourages positive social interaction, active engagement in learning, and self-motivation.

GLOSSARY

Activity-based instruction With this teaching method, activities are used as instructional tools rather than adjuncts or enhancements to instruction. Activity-based instruction involves extensive use of direct student interaction with materials or tasks to achieve learning goals. Proponents emphasize that active participation of the learner promotes student ownership and engagement.

Adaptive switch A device for a computer or other technology that allows a user to access and activate the technology without using the standard method (e.g., if the user cannot easily work a flip switch, perhaps a button switch can be substituted). Adaptive switches come in many varieties and can be designed to fit a specific person's needs.

Alternate keyboard Any keyboard that replaces the standard keyboard for computer access. It does not necessarily have the same features as a standard keyboard but allows access based on an individual's abilities.

Ambulate The ability to move from one place to another.

Anecdotal record A classroom observation strategy that provides descriptive information about (a) students' behavioral patterns or (b) the extent to which students have mastered or applied specific concepts or techniques. The teacher/observer provides a brief description of the students' behavioral pattern or learning experience. For example, several brief anecdotes might be used to illustrate how a student reacts to a particular situation such as a cooperative learning group. Or sketches might show how a student used knowledge from an addition lesson to solve a problem in another subject. Anecdotal records differ from "running records" or "behavioral checklists." Anecdotal records are a distinctly narrative and illustrative method rather than an enumerative or systematic recording of a student's behaviors. Anecdotal records generally require less of the teacher's time and are often completed after the event has occurred (Brophy & Good, 1991).

Appalachian crafts The Appalachian region of the eastern United States extends along the Appalachian Mountains from areas of western Virginia northward through Kentucky, West Virginia, Pennsylvania, and the southern tier of New York State. Rugged and isolating, the mountainous terrain shapes the culture of the region in unique ways. On the one hand, the isolation has given rise to rural poverty and educational equity issues. On the other hand, the seclusion has strengthened a folk culture rich in family traditions and handwork, which has produced some of the most cherished examples of existing Americana. Quilts, woodworking, hand-crafted musical instruments, and myriad other crafts are produced by Appalachian artisans.

Assessment A broad term for the various methods to determine a student's (or school's) academic progress. Assessment is integral to instruction regardless of the pedagogical approach. For example, assessment of didactic instruction may include testing for recognition and recall, while inquiry or holistic instructional approaches may use portfolio scoring with performance rubrics to assess the application of concepts or knowledge. Performance-based assessment as used in a number of states and local districts has met with mixed results.

Assistive technology services   An agency, individual, or program that directly aids an individual with a disability in the selection, acquisition, or use of an assistive technology device.

Authentic assessment   Authentic assessments are designed to correspond as closely as possible to real-world experiences. Problems selected for authentic assessment tasks can be generated by teachers or students and often make use of rubrics to clarify, communicate, and evaluate expectations. Assessing skills in authentic contexts is thought to promote students' capacity for self-monitoring and awareness of personal problem-solving styles and strategies.

BAT keyboard   A type of assistive technology consisting of a keyboard used with one hand. Individuals use different combinations of keys, not unlike "chords" of multiple keys on a piano, to represent the keys on a standard keyboard.

Block scheduling   A change strategy at the secondary-school level that makes use of alternative scheduling to increase the amount of instructional time per class and decrease a student's total number of classes per day. The school day is organized into large blocks of time, usually 75 to 90 minutes, rather than the more traditional 55-minute classes. Block scheduling, as conceived by key proponents, accommodates a variety of instructional strategies and provides time for more planning and interdisciplinary collaboration.

Case method teaching   This pedagogical approach incorporates the examination of specific real life vignettes, scenarios, or narratives into the discussion of and reflection about potential personal actions. The case method relies on five critical stages. First, a student must have a genuine situation or experience to initiate thought. Second, the case must provide enough data to help the learner deal with the specific difficulties this empirical situation presents. Third, the difficulty of new problems must be large enough to challenge thought but contain enough familiar material to shed light on potential solutions. Fourth, the learner is responsible for developing his or her own solutions to the problems through critical thinking. Finally, the learner must have an opportunity to test his or her ideas to make their meaning more clear and to measure validity.

Cerebral palsy   A neurological disorder that affects specific muscles of the body. It ranges from very mild to severe impairment of muscle control, depending on the extent of neurological damage.

Collaboration   See **Team teaching**.

Collegiality   The sharing of educational knowledge and vision among members of a teaching faculty. Productive working relationships among teachers are purported to contribute to school effectiveness by engaging teachers in proactive roles in the construction and coordination of curriculum and instruction. Additionally, collegial interactions can be useful for ongoing professional development and continuous professional assessment.

Constructivism   A term that refers to a collection of educational theories including (among others) discovery learning, generative learning, situated learning, and problem-based learning. These approaches are characterized by a focus on the learner, who actively constructs knowledge and understanding through collaborative, realistic problem solving.

Contextualizing   Conceptual knowledge is not independent of the situations in which it is learned and used. Any presentation of fundamental (and sometimes abstract) theories or concepts in ways that relate to students' everyday life or to their prior knowledge contextualizes learning. This approach allows students to "situate" knowledge within a particular activity, skill, or knowledge base. Knowledge is then useful, rather than disconnected from its applications.

Continuous assessment   Evaluation of students' progress occurs intermittently throughout a learning experience rather than as a single test or performance event following instruction. Continuous assessment benefits both the learner and the instructor. Through incremental evaluation, instructors can gauge student understanding or progress and strategically redesign the approach to meet the needs of the learners. Students' misconceptions or difficulties can be identified early in the learning process; thus, difficulties can be avoided or addressed as they occur.

Cooperative learning   A learning activity in which the instructor structures the assessment and delegates responsibilities to student peer groups to achieve specific tasks. In optimal cooperative learning situations, students are assigned to mixed-ability groups (generally of four to five people) and are given a multifaceted task. Each group member has a designated role to fulfill (e.g., facilitator, recorder, timer, reporter) and all work together to ensure all members complete the instructional goals.

Critical thinking   Critical thinking involves examining information from multiple perspectives before making a decision or coming to a conclusion. One example is the analytic habit of mind that involves defining the key thesis of an argument, evaluating evidence, and assessing appropriate conclusions or logical outcomes.

Curriculum sequencing   A systematic analysis of concepts, materials, and activities that results in an effective ordering that both builds on previous learning and challenges students to use existing knowledge to acquire new understandings. Effective curriculum sequencing connects various concepts and ideas to support thorough understanding.

Disability   The reduction of function of some part of the body (e.g., loss of sight, or a learning disability).

Due process rights   Rules that ensure the informed participation, consent, and adequate procedures for parents and students regarding the child's evaluation, program placement, and educational plan in special education.

Experience-based instruction   Based on the work of educational philosopher John Dewey, experiential education emphasizes the central role of the student as active learner in the instructional process. Dewey stressed that experiences can be cognitive as well as physical in nature and that, most important, grounding concepts in experiences contextualizes their meaning and promotes complex understandings and the desire to continue learning.

Firewall   This term refers to software that serves as an electronic barrier for a networked or desktop computing system. Firewalls are used for information security, particularly in school systems. For example, a firewall may prevent students from accessing Internet sites that may contain objectionable materials. Firewalls have limitations, and many students who are proficient with technology can circumvent the strictures set up by firewall software.

Free and appropriate education   The federally mandated right of all students regardless of disability to an education that is appropriate and provided free of any cost to the parents or guardians.

Full inclusion plan   The placement of a student with disabilities in a regular education classroom for all of his or her classes.

Guided discovery An instructional approach that focuses on the acquisition of knowledge through exploration that is grounded in an understanding of previously acquired basic concepts of the subject. Proponents of this approach claim students draw on a foundation of knowledge to apply learning to specific examples through personal exploration and discovery.

Hands-on activities See **Activity-based instruction**.

Heterogeneous grouping A method of assigning students to instructional activities or classes by varying abilities rather than by similar characteristics or same-level abilities. The rationale in support of multiple-ability grouping is that each student has the opportunity to contribute to the group and to learn to value the unique contributions of others.

Inclusion A term that refers to the practice in schools of placing a special education student in a regular education classroom setting. Specific services or supports that enable the special-needs student to fully participate in the class (such as a signer for a deaf child) must also be provided in an "inclusive" setting.

Individualized Education Plan (IEP) A mandatory written plan that must be developed for each student in special education every year to outline the student's educational goals and objectives, as well as the special education services that will be provided, and to provide a time line for when and where services will take place.

Individuals with Disabilities Education Act (IDEA) Federal legislation regarding individuals with disabilities, which guarantees them the following from birth to 21: due process rights, an education in the least restrictive environment, nondiscriminatory assessment, an individualized education plan (IEP), confidentiality and the right to privacy regarding records, the services of a parent surrogate if needed, and a free and appropriate education until age 21.

Integrated software program Commercially available computer software package that contains several types of programs such as a word processing program, a spreadsheet, a database, and a graphics or drawing program. Examples of such integrated packages include Microsoft Works, Microsoft Office, and Corel Suite.

Inquiry approach An instructional approach that allows students to explore a situation, make inductive judgments, and, through discovery, define underlying concepts. In pure inquiry, these concepts are explained, labeled, or defined by the teacher after students have worked independently to describe the phenomena. By contrast, in guided inquiry, students are taught basic concepts prior to exploration.

INTASC The Interstate New Teacher Assessment and Support Consortium is sponsored by the council of Chief State School Officers. More than half the states have adopted or adapted the INTASC standards as part of teacher certification requirements.

Integrated instruction An individual classroom teacher draws on theoretical or conceptual perspectives from a variety of disciplines. For example, students reading *The Great Gatsby* might explore the use of irony in the plot while also studying the social or political implications of Prohibition on the events in the novel.

Interdisciplinary instruction Curriculum that integrates the perspectives of different content areas into instruction on a common topic. Working as a collaborative team, teachers present students with the themes or concepts that connect knowledge within the different subject areas. For example, history and science teachers might collaborate on the theme of inventions that changed America.

Internship Several states have comprehensive support programs for new teachers. Teachers involved in internship programs generally hold initial certification and are assigned to a faculty support team. This specialized support assists the teacher during the initial year with instructional planning, assessment strategies, and periodic performance reviews. Successful completion of an internship usually culminates in enhanced certification status, depending on individual state certification requirements.

KERA Passed in 1990, the Kentucky Education Reform Act is an example of systemic reform because of its simultaneous emphasis on major change in the areas of finance, governance, and curriculum. In the late 1980s, 66 property-poor districts sued the state superintendent for inequities in education and won (*Rose v. Council for Better Education, Inc.*). The Kentucky Supreme Court's ruling that Kentucky's public school system was unconstitutional prompted the legislative and executive branches of state government to reconstruct the entire educational system.

Kid Works An integrated software package designed specifically for use by children. In addition to a word processor, a spreadsheet, a database, and a drawing program, the package is often bundled with educational software such as an interactive phonics program, and reading and writing tutorials for young children (http://www.mwcdrom.com).

Learning disability (LD) Problems in learning that do not directly result from a disadvantaged background, mental retardation, sensory impairments, or behavioral disorders are termed learning disabilities. Extremely varied and complex, these deficiencies include specific difficulties in learning to read, write, calculate, or solve problems. More students are identified for special educational services for LD than any other disability.

Least restrictive environment The federally mandated right of students with disabilities to be placed in the least restrictive education setting that will meet their needs (e.g., regular education classroom with pullout to a resource room for math). A continuum of settings exists including, but not limited to, regular class placement with few or no supportive services, full-time special class, and hospital or institution.

Mainstreaming The practice of including students with disabilities in the regular education setting as much as appropriate during the school day.

Mastery level A term for proficiency associated with the mastery learning approach, which stresses individualizing instruction. Mastery learning is made possible by goal specification and incremental assessment. Since intended outcomes are made clear and their assessment sought, the need for self-pacing and other forms of individualization becomes apparent. In mastery environments, students do not progress to the next level of knowledge or skill acquisition without demonstrating full proficiency at the previous one.

Mathematics manipulatives Math manipulatives are physical objects that represent a mathematical idea or concept. Students can observe or arrange the physical objects for inductive or deductive activities that help them understand mathematical ideas or concepts for which they cannot readily construct mental models. Examples of math manipulatives are "geo-boards" that have rows of pegs and elastic bands that children stretch into various shapes and pattern blocks sets containing wooden or plastic shapes coded with specific colors that can be identified and arranged into various configurations to illustrate concepts such as a triangle or a square.

Mentor A master teacher who works with a novice teacher or in a peer review or professional development capacity to facilitate the acquisition or refinement of teaching skills. A mentor can function in both an informal (at a peer's request) or formal capacity (as in some internship programs) and takes the role of knowledgeable guide vis-à-vis the learner. Research suggests that mentors benefit from their helping role through an affirmation of their professionalism and skill as well as through the energizing effects of working with eager, though less experienced colleagues.

Moebius syndrome A rare genetic disorder that is characterized by several factors, including facial paralysis resulting in the inability to smile or frown and often to blink or move the eyes from side to side.

Multidisciplinary transition team A team composed of individuals with personal or professional relations to a special-needs student, who work together to make plans and address issues related to the successful transition from one environment to another (e.g., from elementary school to middle school).

Multiple intelligences According to educational theorist Howard Gardner, measuring human potential solely by linguistic and mathematical/logical assessments is limiting. He posits several different "human intelligences," including verbal/linguistic, musical, spatial, interpersonal, bodily-kinesthetic, intrapersonal, and naturalist. Supporters of Gardner advocate the importance of using all the intelligences when developing curriculum and instruction.

Multi-age/multi-ability classroom model The philosophy stems from a position statement of the National Association for the Education of Young Children. It promotes the importance of teachers working with the whole child—his or her physical, social, emotional and cognitive dimensions—within an integrated curriculum. Children engage in hands-on, active learning, rather than passive, paper-and-pencil activities (as described in McIntyre & Kyle [1996], *The Review of Education Research on* KERA).

NBPTS Founded in 1987, the National Board for Professional Teaching Standards consists of a 63-member board of directors, the majority of whom are classroom teachers. The board's mission is to recognize accomplished teachers who can effectively enhance student learning and clearly demonstrate what they know and are able to do based on rigorous standards. To date, hundreds of K–12 teachers have become nationally board certified through a strictly voluntary assessment process.

O'Keeffe, Georgia Prominent American painter (1887–1986) known for her close-up, colorful paintings of flowers.

Outcome-based instruction Related to competency-based education, this is a teaching approach in which teachers first develop a clear definition of what is consequential for students to learn and then plan curriculum according to the desired end results. All students must demonstrate their mastery of the specified outcomes.

Pattern blocks Geometric mathematics manipulatives that are uniformly color coded. Triangles are green, trapezoids are red, squares are orange, rhombuses are tan, and hexagons are yellow. Children can learn to conceptualize not only the shapes but higher-order concepts such as sorting and categorizing.

Pedagogy The art or method of teaching. Pedagogy is defined by choices involving the selection or combination of the basic underlying psychological, social, and philosophical theories and methods of teaching.

Peer review An evaluation process that uses review and commentary by "equals" (for example, classmates) rather than external judgments to assess the value of work. Used by teachers and students alike, peer review has often been implemented as a major component of the evaluation process.

Performance-based assessment The assessment of understanding and/or mastery of a given concept, skill, or procedure is demonstrated through direct application to a specific, demonstrable task rather than through interim exams that measure declarative knowledge.

Physical disability Any physical or health problem that impairs an individual from completing a task or activity so that specialized equipment is necessary to function normally in society.

Pollock, Jackson American abstract expressionist (1912–1956) noted for his drip technique of painting.

Problem-based learning (PBL) First developed some 20 years ago to address the complexities of applying knowledge in preclinical medicine that, at the time, primarily used traditional lecture style teaching. Using PBL, learning is organized around realistic tasks in a field, and students explain, define, or apply knowledge in the context of true-to-life or simulated situations.

Professional development The process of continuous study, evaluation, and improvement performed by an educator to refine and enhance his or her performance.

Prosthetic legs Artificial devices used when an individual has lost or been born without all or part of his or her legs.

RAM There are two types of computer memory: random access memory (RAM) and read-only memory (ROM). RAM is specifically used by the computer to store new data (such as a word processing file document you may be typing) and to run specific programs (such as your word processing program). Data and program instructions are entered into the computer's central processing unit and then it is "accessed" by RAM when instructed to do so by the user (i.e., one double-clicks on a program icon on the desktop, and the RAM executes the command).

Reading Recovery Program Reading Recovery is an early intervention program designed by Marie Clay to assist children in first grade who are having difficulty learning to read and write. Its goal is to train teachers to make skilled teaching decisions that enable the at-risk reader to make accelerated progress and to become a competent, independent reader in approximately 12–20 weeks.

Reflective practitioner This term, introduced in Donald Schoen's (1986) book *The Reflective Practitioner*, now commonly refers to the practice of constantly reviewing and evaluating one's own effectiveness as a teacher and continually improving or adapting teaching methods. A philosophical basis for reflective practice is found in John Dewey's (1934) book *How We Think*.

Renoir, Pierre Auguste French Impressionist painter and sculptor (1841–1919).

Resource teacher A special education teacher who gives instruction to a variety of students for part or all of the day.

Restructuring In recent years this term has become so widespread in its reference to reform efforts that its meaning has become ambiguous. However, early advocates of school restructuring contend its original meaning is that decisions should be made by those closest to the problems needing to be resolved. For example, curriculum decisions once reserved for administrators should be based on shared decision making involving faculty and parents.

Rubric A clearly defined set of standards used to operationalize criteria for achievement of skills at various levels of proficiency. For example, criteria to demonstrate skills at beginning, advanced, or fully proficient levels comprise a basic rubric. Rubrics appraise performance rather than assign grades. While rubrics can delineate a performance scale that can fairly assess achievement, their use in some contexts been controversial because of inconsistent application of the performance indicators.

School-based decision making (SBDM) An increasingly popular method of school governance that assigns a key role in school decision making directly to a council composed of administrators, parents, teachers, and community members. Proponents of SBDM feel the faculty and parental involvement results in a more effective schooling for students through shared responsibility for education.

Self-contained program A special education program in which students receive all of their instruction in a single classroom and are not mainstreamed into regular education classes.

Team teaching Teachers work together in pairs or groups to develop integrated lessons drawing from their various knowledge and experience. The lessons may then be taught by each teacher individually in his or her own classroom or by several teachers to one common class, with each teacher presenting the material from his or her particular discipline in a team environment.

Thematic teaching Focusing the curriculum around a group of themes, often linking each new theme to the previous one, and presenting each skill or concept to be learned within the context of the theme being studied. For example, use of the theme "conflict and consensus" can tie together historical events over the course of several decades and political contexts in U.S. history.

Tracking Disparate schooling for individual students, maintained by assigning students to a particular long-term educational program of a set level of academic ability, based on an early general assessment of the students' learning capacities. Many educational reformers seek to eliminate tracking from school programs based on the belief that tracking permanently labels students and does not provide the opportunity for them to achieve at their highest level.

Wide-area network (WAN) A communications network that connects computers at geographically separate locations. For example, all of the computers and printers in a school building may be connected on a local area network (LAN), but to use the Internet, those computers must be connected to a wide area network (WAN) that links to communication servers and electronic information (such as the World Wide Web) outside the school building.

Wyeth, Andrew Newell American painter born in 1917 in Chadds Ford, Pennsylvania; son of the illustrator N. C. Wyeth, he is noted for a highly realistic style.